BEYOND
MEDIOCRITY

TRANSFORMATIVE FRAMEWORKS

For Business, Career, and Life Mastery

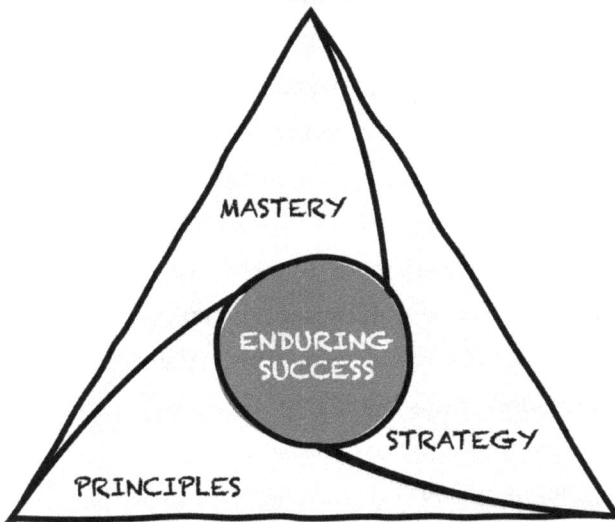

The Battlefield Wisdom.
Outmaneuver. Outthink. Outperform.

Sudhir Kadam

Copyright Notice

ISBN: 979-8-9986805-1-9
First Released May 2025

Gratitude

To my Mother (Tara) and Father (Balkrishna)

To my Wife (Tejaswi) and Son (Aditya)

To Shri Radha and Shri Krishna

Table of Contents

The Inspiration

My journey with the *Bhagavad Gita* began when my brother, Subodh (affectionately, *Bhai*), gifted me an English translation and urged me to read Chapter 14. I was in the 9th grade then and couldn't fathom the profoundness of its verses, but it sparked a curiosity within me.

Years later, my good friend, Dr. Bansal, asked me to review the English translation of his Hindi rendition of the *Gita*. This turned into an immersive experience that lasted over eight months, deepening my connection to its wisdom. I struggled with finding the right words to capture the depth and flow of his narration, which made the *Gita* come alive in a whole new way.

Two years later, a fellow IITian, Sri, presented me with his English translation of the *Gita*, written in the same poetic meter as the Sanskrit original. His poetic approach made me realize just how many ways the *Gita* can be interpreted for different audiences.

I thought to myself: Could this wisdom be shared with the uninitiated in a way that is simple, accessible, and resonates with everyday life?

As a Silicon Valley venture builder and strategy advisor for growth acceleration, market expansion, and innovation programs for startups and enterprises, I strive to distill knowledge into actionable frameworks. I believe that learning becomes truly impactful only when it is simplified, structured, and applicable to real-world contexts.

This book applies that same approach to the *Gita*—extracting its relevant insights and organizing them into practical tools for readers—entrepreneurs, executives, seekers—to apply in business, career, and life. If people find value in this research, I hope the message will spread organically—through word of mouth, shared wisdom, and lived experience.

Thank you for embarking on this journey to transcend mediocrity and achieve mastery.

Sudhir Kadam
sudhir@fyda.net

Note: Interpreting the *Gita* in the context of the modern world can lead to different perspectives, and so this interpretation may differ from others. What truly matters is how these teachings are applied to help us navigate life, business, and career in a meaningful way.

A Gateway to Mastery

Why do teams fail to execute? Why do high-potential people stall? Why do ventures lose momentum?

Why do promising careers plateau? Why do relationships fail? Why does life feel like a tunnel?

The signs are everywhere: drift, confusion, overload, and burnout. It's a defining challenge of our time. Nowhere is this more visible than in startups, where founders juggle nonstop decisions while fearing they're missing the next big thing.

Not knowing what to hold on to, what to let go of, or what to move toward. That's the trap of **mediocrity**.

So how do we move from mediocrity to **mastery**?

The answer lies in an ancient battlefield dialogue captured in the timeless Indian scripture—the *Bhagavad Gita* (or the *Gita*, for short). A conversation that symbolizes clarity and decisive action in the line of duty.

This book blends these timeless insights with the language of modern life and entrepreneurship. It equips you with visual and mental models infused with practical strategies to pursue mastery in business and in life.

Important Note: *Do not skip the introductory sections. They introduce core concepts and visual frameworks. Think of them as the compass to enrich your* ***transformative journey!***

The Bhagavad Gita Unveiled

For over two millennia, the *Bhagavad Gita* (also called the *Gita*) has stood as a beacon of wisdom, guiding seekers from all walks of life. It is a divine dialogue between Arjun, the warrior prince, and Krishna, his philosopher-guide, set on the battlefield of Kurukshetra in India—a setting that symbolizes the inner battles we all face. Emerging from the epic *Mahabharat*, this battlefield dialogue offers a universal philosophy for navigating life's complexities. A philosophy that illuminates the human quest for purpose, clarity, and action.

The Battle of Kurukshetra was fought between two factions of the Kuru dynasty—the Pandavas and the Kauravas. The Pandavas, rightful heirs to the throne, were denied their kingdom by their cousins, the Kauravas, leading to years of conflict and failed diplomatic efforts. When peace failed, war loomed, and Arjun, the mightiest Pandava warrior, faced a crisis: fight his kin or abandon his duty. On the eve of battle, he laid down his weapons, questioning the morality of war and the purpose of his existence.

At this pivotal moment, Krishna, Arjun's mentor and charioteer, delivered the divine discourse of the *Gita*. Through this dialogue, Krishna addresses Arjun's turmoil while illuminating timeless dilemmas: duty, morality, fear, attachment, and the pursuit of purpose. The *Gita* is a text to live, not just read, offering clarity for our own crossroads.

Krishna, the Universal Consciousness

The *Gita* delves into profound questions about life, death, duty, and reality. Krishna, who delivers the discourse to Arjun, represents the dynamic principle of cosmic intelligence, guiding all beings toward their highest potential. His teachings in *the Gita* are not bound by culture or belief but offer wisdom on the nature of life and self-mastery. Think of him as the conscious spark of clarity and action that cuts through confusion, whether in a boardroom or a personal crisis.

In Business and Leadership, Krishna reflects strategic adaptability and ethical decision-making—tools to lead with purpose and rally teams under pressure.

In Career and Professional Growth, Krishna stands for resilience and focus, driving disciplined effort toward meaningful impact.

In Personal Life and Relationships, Krishna offers balance and empathy, deepening connections and steadying us through change.

In Creativity and Innovation, Krishna represents the free flow of inspiration and Divine play (*Leela*). His boundless nature—warrior, strategist, musician, and philosopher—ignites inspiration and creative spontaneity.

Whether you see Krishna as a metaphor for higher awareness, an archetype of enlightened leadership, or a mentor, the *Gita's* wisdom speaks to fundamental truths, enabling us to move beyond fear and confusion toward a life of clarity, action, and fulfillment.

The Transformative Power of the Gita

Whether grappling with career dilemmas, ethical quandaries, or personal struggles, when you stand at life's crossroads, searching for answers, the *Gita* serves as a lighthouse, offering clarity and resolve, as it did for Arjun. This book takes excerpts from the timeless wisdom of the *Gita* to help you navigate the modern challenges of life by turbocharging your ability to approach challenges with confidence and clarity.

The *Gita* teaches us the art of selfless action, showing how detachment from outcomes can enhance productivity and reduce stress. It explains the path of knowledge that helps us align with a larger vision of life. It reveals the power of belief to help us move forward with faith instead of fear. It teaches us discernment through the path of intellect to gain the clarity to choose wisely and act with purpose. Through the path of meditative stillness, it helps us quiet the mind, sharpen focus, and cultivate presence even amid chaos.

Each chapter makes these paths actionable to reshape thinking, decision-making, and growth. By internalizing its teachings, you will find yourself approaching conflicts with greater wisdom, handling stress with a calm mind, and unlocking the potential to live a life of deep fulfillment and excellence.

The wisdom of the *Gita* is not to be passively absorbed but actively lived. Let it inspire and challenge you to rise beyond limitations.

The Structure of this Book

Each chapter begins with a concise summary of the main teachings and then relates them to business and personal life with modern challenges. To ground the teachings in practicality, two key verses from the chapter are presented, accompanied by their real-world applications.

This book uses triangular frameworks to simplify each chapter's philosophical concepts into three core dimensions that shape the teachings, with its unifying theme in the center. This makes the concepts clear, helping you apply them to your own context.

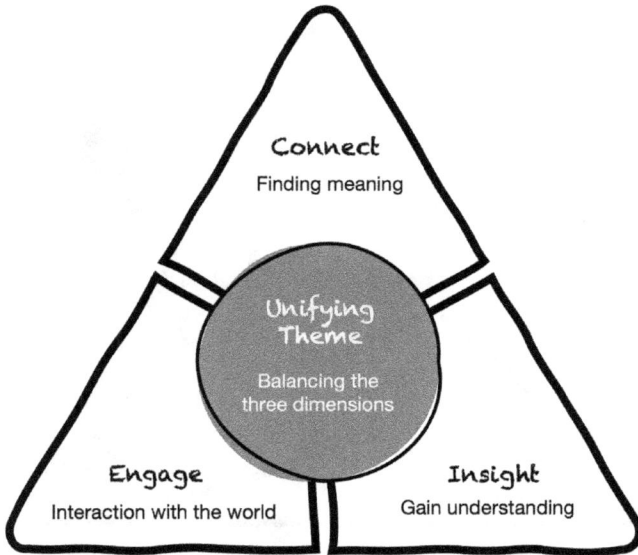

Finally, each chapter concludes with the visual framework adapted for entrepreneurs and business leaders, providing actionable insights and strategies to integrate these teachings into business and professional growth.

The Gita's Wisdom for Business Mastery

For every chapter, you will find frameworks for entrepreneurs and business leaders. These are not mental models for businesses to operate from a position of clarity, impact, and mastery.

Each framework offers a distinct yet interconnected lesson—progressing from the inner conflicts of leadership to the strategic execution of vision, from understanding human nature to mastering the external forces of competition and change. The culmination is *Mastery* in business—the state where leaders and organizations operate with absolute freedom, purpose, and resilience, making bold decisions while staying untouched by fleeting successes or failures.

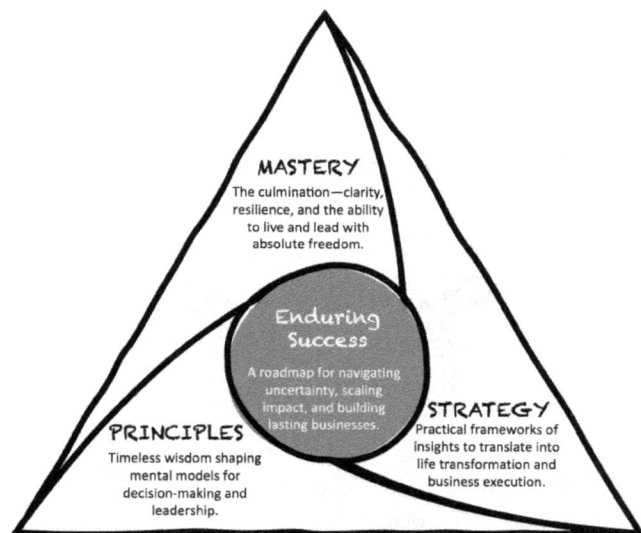

Whether you're an entrepreneur scaling a startup, an executive leading transformation, or a strategist shaping the future, these frameworks provide a roadmap to navigate uncertainty with wisdom, act with conviction, and build a business that not only succeeds but endures.

5-3-1 Framework: A Foundational Lens

In both life and business, we often find ourselves caught in cycles of uncertainty. While we seek purpose and direction, our perception is shaped by forces that either guide us forward or hold us back.

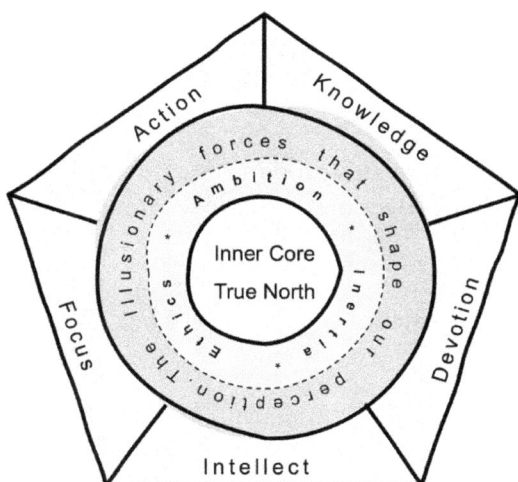

Action · Knowledge · Focus · Devotion · Intellect

forces that shape our perception

Illusionary · Ambition · Ethics · The perception

Inner Core
True North

For those who are new to the concept of the *Gita*, this 5-3-1 framework is a foundational lens, a prelude to the journey of *Gita's* deeper teachings and core principles you will encounter in this book.

At the core of every individual lies an **Inner Core**, just as every business has its **True North**—the essence that must be rediscovered and aligned. Yet, this clarity is often obscured by **three forces** that shape our perception—sometimes guiding us, other times misleading us. By understanding these forces and consciously applying the **five disciplines**, we can break through illusions and move toward sustainable growth, both personally and professionally.

There are two distinct views of the 5-3-1 framework, one for personal development in career or relationships, and one for business leaders and entrepreneurs. While fundamentally the framework remains the same, the lens changes for context relevance.

5-3-1 Framework: The Personal Path Within

1 Inner Core: Your true self—the eternal part—your "True North."

3 Forces *(Primal Energies)* that Shape How We See the World:

- Ethics: *How we decide right from wrong*
  - ○ Helpful when balanced: Gives us clear principles
  - ○ Challenging when extreme: Becomes rigid rules

- Ambition: *Our desire to achieve*
  - ○ Helpful when balanced: Motivates growth
  - ○ Challenging when extreme: Becomes endless wanting

- Inertia: *Our resistance to change*
  - ○ Helpful when balanced: Provides stability
  - ○ Challenging when extreme: Keeps us stuck

When imbalanced, we are trapped in illusion, hindering clarity.

5 Paths to Break Through Illusion to Find the Balance:

- Knowledge: Understanding the changing landscape
  - ○ *Continuous learning → Staying relevant*

- Focus: Being fully present in whatever you do
  - ○ *Laser attention → Whole-minded engagement*

- Devotion: Acting from love and commitment, not obligation
  - ○ *Passion for the work → Dedication beyond results*

- Intellect: Making clear decisions based on wisdom
  - ○ *Filtering noise → Aligned decisions*

- Action: Doing your duty without attachment to results
  - ○ *Doing what's needed → Owning the outcome*

5-3-1 Framework: The Business Compass

1 True North: Company's purpose (why) that guides decisions.

3 Forces *(Primal Energies)* that Shape Business Clarity:

- Ethics: Questions: *Upholding values vs. survival risk*
  - When balanced: Builds trust and reputation
  - When imbalanced: Can limit innovation and growth

- Ambition: *Choosing drive vs. obsession.*
  - When balanced: Drives progress and achievement
  - When imbalanced: Leads to overreach and burnout

- Inertia: *Slowing down vs. unwilling to change.*
  - When balanced: Provides stability and consistency
  - When imbalanced: Resists necessary change

Imbalance in these forces blurs long-term vision.

5 Key Disciplines for Business Success:

- Knowledge: Turning innovation into adaptability
  - *Continuous learning, seeing patterns, new insights*

- Focus: Maintaining persistent clarity that enables agility
  - *Staying centered when faced with market disruptions*

- Devotion: Building culture that creates commitment
  - *Internal alignment that translates to customer value*

- Strategy: The "how"—roadmap that guides the execution
  - *Setting direction with foresight and insight*

- Execution: Moving from action to meaningful impact
  - *Doing the right things and executing with faith, without fear*

Chapter 1
The Inner Conflict

The first chapter of the *Gita*, sets the stage for the entire discourse. Arjun, a mighty warrior prepared for battle, stands on the threshold of action, facing an intense moral and emotional conflict on the battlefield of Kurukshetra. As he looks across the battlefield and sees his own kin, teachers, and friends as adversaries, he is overcome with grief and uncertainty. He questions the purpose of war, the morality of violence, and the implications of his actions.

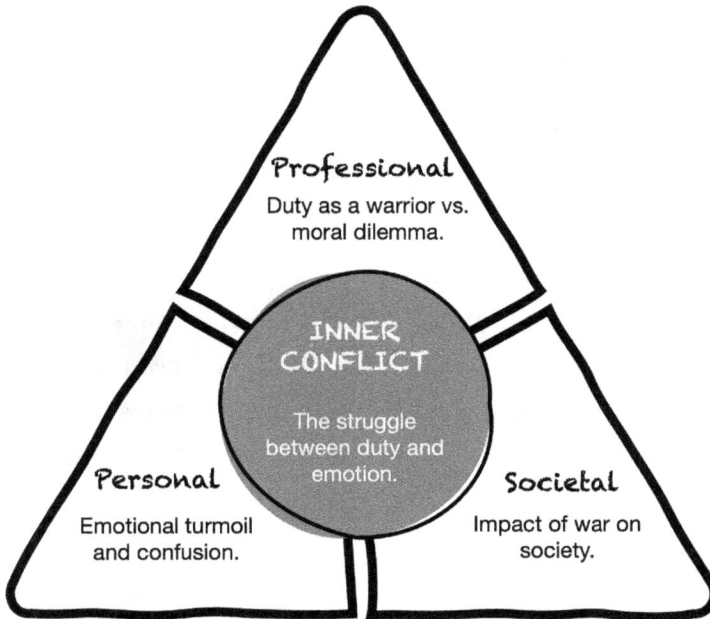

This moment of pause, hesitation, and confusion is not weakness. It is a human condition. At some point in life, we all find ourselves in the middle of a battlefield of choices, where logic, emotion, ethics, and responsibility collide. The *Gita* begins here because **clarity cannot emerge until conflict is acknowledged.**

This chapter highlights the root cause of all suffering—our struggle to reconcile external expectations with internal conviction. Arjun's despair mirrors the dilemmas we face in our lives when confronted with difficult choices. The fundamental teaching here is the importance of righteous action or duty (*Dharma*) even in the face of difficulty.

➤ *Decision paralysis isn't solved by intellect alone—it needs emotional alignment and moral clarity.*

Every decision we make creates a ripple within us and around us. Our current reality is shaped by past actions, and the future will be shaped by what we choose now. When our personal ambitions often collide with ethical boundaries. Our success may come at the cost of self-respect, relationships, or long-term meaning.

In high-stakes situations, when driven by fear, pressure, or ego, we may delay decisions or avoid action altogether. Arjun's predicament is a mirror to our own hesitation. But inaction is not neutral—it creates its own consequences. Indecision, hesitation, and emotional turmoil can lead to paralysis in action, causing further distress.

➤ *Indecision is a form of inaction—and it carries a cost.*

This is the moment for a mental shift to transform conflict into resolution. This lesson is timeless: **our strength in tough moments shapes our path.** It is about opening ourselves to seek inner alignment to face life's challenges with composure and conviction.

This chapter isn't about the grief of a warrior—it is about the ethical, moral, or personal dilemmas and struggles we all face. It reminds us that growth begins with honest questions; wisdom, courage, and action then light the way forward.

The Calm Before the Storm

Chapter 1, Verses 21–22: "Arjun, the mighty warrior, spoke to Krishna: Position my chariot between the two armies. Let me see those who stand eager for battle—those I must fight in this great struggle."

Arjun's request is deceptively simple yet charged with tension. This is the last moment of clarity before the weight of war shatters his certainty. He is armored, armed, and outwardly resolute. His body is ready, but his mind has not yet reckoned with the consequences.

This moment is universal: the breath before the plunge, the instance before a life-altering decision. An athlete poised at the starting block. A leader about to announce a painful restructuring. An entrepreneur seconds before a pitch that could define their future.

➤ *Readiness is not the same as resolution.*

Arjun's command, *"Place me where I can see my enemies,"* masks a deeper question: *"Do I truly want to see them?"* Because to look is to confront not just opponents but relationships. How often do we charge forward before reckoning with the consequence? **The battlefield is external, but the war is within.**

Krishna, silent for now, positions the chariot for Arjun to confront what courage truly demands—not just the will to fight, but the strength to question.

▶ *Certainty is easy—until the stakes become visible.*

This is the moment to pause—before the first arrow flies, before the irreversible begins.

Collapse Before Clarity

Chapter 1, Verse 47: "Arjun sat down on the seat of his chariot, his mind overwhelmed with sorrow, having set aside his bow and arrows."

This is not a pause but a collapse. Not of body, but of spirit. The warrior who never feared death is now paralyzed by duty. The leader who always knew his next move is suddenly empty. This verse marks the lowest point in Arjun's journey—where purpose, pride, and strength all fall away.

And Krishna remains silent.

Because real wisdom doesn't speak until confusion is acknowledged. In that silence, Arjun crumbles emotionally. And from that collapse, the journey begins.

▶ *Sometimes the breakdown is the breakthrough.*

Every meaningful transformation begins with this moment—when we put down the tools, the roles, and the masks. When we finally
24

admit, "I *don't know what to do.*" That's when true wisdom finds space to enter.

Entrepreneurial Framework 1:

The Leadership Crisis: Facing Tough Decisions

The hallmark of an entrepreneur is the ability to confront emotional turmoil in the line of duty, even when the path is difficult or unpleasant.

Theme: Emotional resilience by overcoming self-doubt and fear to make high-stakes decisions.

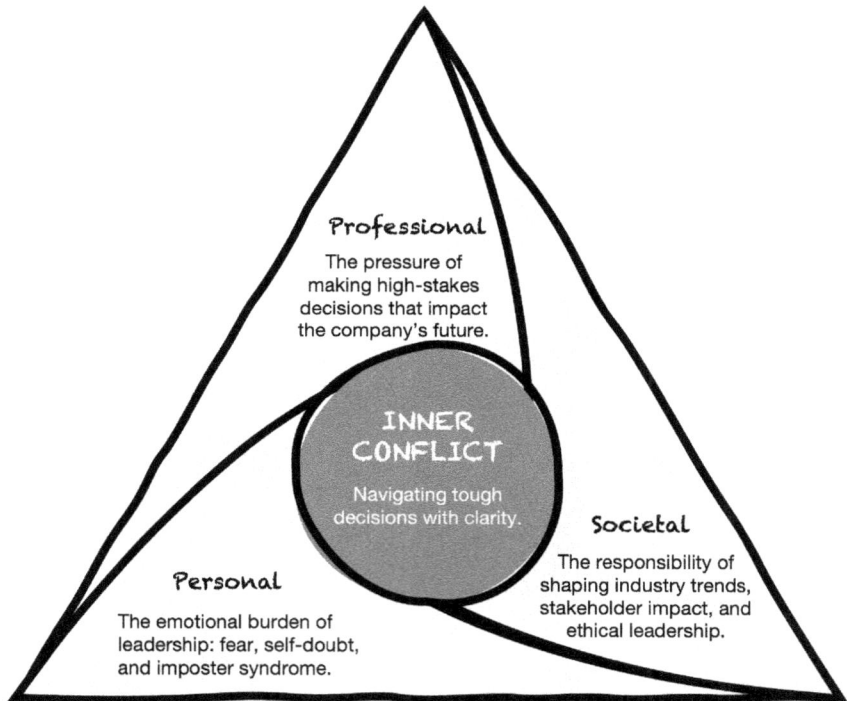

Professional
The pressure of making high-stakes decisions that impact the company's future.

INNER CONFLICT
Navigating tough decisions with clarity.

Societal
The responsibility of shaping industry trends, stakeholder impact, and ethical leadership.

Personal
The emotional burden of leadership: fear, self-doubt, and imposter syndrome.

Business Insight:

Every entrepreneur faces moments of self-doubt, ethical dilemmas, and decision paralysis—whether in taking risks, pivoting strategies, or handling crises. When pressure, uncertainty, and stakes collide, clarity doesn't arrive instantly. Leaders must confront their inner fears and conflicts, balancing personal emotions, professional duties, and societal impact.

➤ *Collapse isn't weakness—it's the clearing ground for real leadership.*

These are moments of pause, not failure—they are **invitations to reframe and seek new perspective**, knowing that every challenge carries its solution within. In the quiet between breaths, in the space between actions, wisdom whispers. This is not unusual in the rollercoaster of business—this "is" the journey. Leadership begins when we stop posturing and start listening. Acting with clarity, especially when the stakes are high, may mean cutting costs to preserve the mission, pivoting with conviction, or protecting people over vanity metrics.

➤ *Leadership begins when clarity is earned—not assumed.*

Imagine an entrepreneur navigating a pivot during a market downturn: grappling with uncertainty, managing team morale, and questioning every move. The pressure to play it safe can be overwhelming. But clarity doesn't come from avoidance. It comes from facing discomfort. Strong leaders don't retreat to comfort—they return to purpose and act from there.

Krishna remained silent for a reason. True wisdom waits until we admit confusion and let righteous action shine as the anchor.

Action Step: When doubt strikes, leaders ask, "What must be done now?" "What am I avoiding emotionally?" "What is expected of me?" Let discomfort guide you, and clarity lead your return.

Once **conflict** is confronted, the next step is to resolve it with **strategic clarity**, which is explored in the next chapter.

Chapter 2
Steady Through the Storm

The second chapter of the *Gita* marks a shift from confusion to clarity. Krishna begins to respond to Arjun's inner crisis by offering a foundational wisdom that transforms how we engage with the world.

It marks the beginning of Krishna's teachings on knowledge (*Jnana*), action (*Karma*), and the path to liberation from inner clarity *(Moksha)*.

Krishna reveals that we often get entangled in the relentless pursuit of wealth, status, and external validation. Life's ultimate aim is not to be shackled by material attachments but to rise above them, through awareness and purpose, for inner freedom. True success lies in inner stability, not just outward wins.

▶ *Inner steadiness is the starting point of outer excellence.*

Our world is influenced by three forces or energies (*Gunas*) that shape our minds and manifest as traits. *Sattva* brings ethics and clarity. *Rajas* drives ambition and restlessness. *Tamas* creates inertia and confusion. These forces are constantly at play in our minds, our environments, and our organizations.

When *Sattva* dominates, we act with clarity, calm, and compassion. When *Rajas* takes over, we chase outcomes, recognition, or speed. When *Tamas* prevails, we apply brakes to slow down to anchor.

Recognizing their patterns of manifestation creates self-awareness. Leaders should be able to identify when the ambition of Rajas risks burnout, when the stagnation of Tamas slows momentum, or when the idealism of Sattva loses grip on execution. The goal isn't to suppress these qualities but to become conscious of their influence and wisely bring the right balance of energies.

➤ *Awareness isn't escape—it's intelligent engagement.*

A core lesson in this chapter is **equanimity** (*Samatva*)—the ability to stay steady through success and failure, pleasure and pain. It shows that clinging to outcomes breeds suffering, while wisdom lies in detaching from the result and staying devoted to the effort. This echoes the principle of the path of action (*Karma Yoga*).

➤ *Detach from the result—stay devoted to the effort.*

Today, fear and doubt often stem from attaching self-worth to titles, wealth, or digital applause ("likes"). By seeing our value beyond these fleeting tags and shifting metrics, we build the spine to withstand setbacks. Challenges become opportunities, not sources of despair or reasons to retreat. Setbacks don't define us—they refine us.

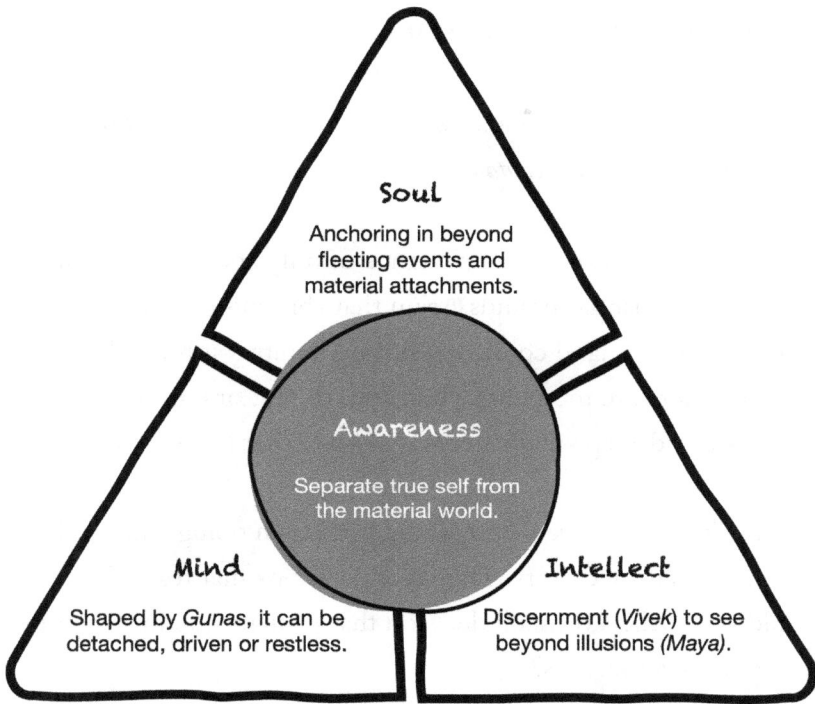

```
                    Soul
              Anchoring in beyond
               fleeting events and
              material attachments.

                  Awareness

              Separate true self from
                the material world.

      Mind                        Intellect
Shaped by Gunas, it can be    Discernment (Vivek) to see
detached, driven or restless.  beyond illusions (Maya).
```

This chapter also mentions the discipline of intellect (*Buddhi Yoga*), guiding decisions with wisdom over whim. In a world buzzing with noise, endless alerts, trending opinions, and the pressure to react, it is the discipline of intellect that can help cut through the distractions to ground us in reason.

➤ *In a busy and noisy world, pause to listen inward.*

The path of intellect relies on discernment over emotional sway. By practicing it, we separate rational thought from knee-jerk reactions. Picture a leader choosing strategy over panic in a crisis. Reason rules, outcomes improve. By separating impulse from insight, the path of intellect allows us to act with conviction, anchored in reason. We move with intention, not insecurity.

Stand Up for What Is Right and Act

Chapter 2, Verse 33: "If you will not fight this righteous war, then you will fail in your duty and lose your reputation as a warrior."

This verse emphasizes the importance of duty and action in the face of adversity. Krishna reminds Arjun that shirking responsibility in moments that demand courage is not neutrality—it is a failure of purpose. There are moments when fear, doubt, or emotional distress tempt us to sidestep what's necessary—whether in work or life.

Business leaders are frequently caught between doing what feels right and what's necessary. They face decisions that test this tension: Should you make a difficult decision that protects the mission but may strain relationships?

A manager may have to let go of an underperforming employee despite personal goodwill. A founder may have to pivot away from the current strategy to save the company's core mission. These are not easy calls—but they are necessary ones. Avoiding them could lead to greater problems later.

▶ *Avoiding discomfort may feel safer in the short term—but does it serve the long term?*

The message here is about fortitude. It's about standing firm in your role for what must be done, not acting out of emotions or ego. The reputation that matters is built on consistency of purpose, not popularity. Facing challenges head-on, even with uncertainty, builds resilience and character.

Equilibrium in All Situations

Chapter 2, Verse 38: "Treat pleasure and pain, gain and loss, victory and defeat alike. Prepare for the battle ahead."

This verse articulates the principle of equanimity—it's about presence and emotional balance that remains steadfast, regardless of outcome.

Life is a pendulum; circumstances swing between success and failure, happiness and distress. When we peg ourselves to wins measured by career peaks, bank balances, and relationships, euphoria hits when they soar, despair when they dip. Equanimity cuts that cord, steadies the mind. Act with integrity, give your best, and let go of the emotional swings attached to the outcomes.

► *Equanimity is not indifference—it's engagement without emotional volatility.*

Think of a professional navigating promotions and layoffs, an entrepreneur riding profit or loss, or an athlete meeting victory or defeat. Fixating on these swings steals our inner peace. But the leader who stays unshaken in adversity decides with reason, not panic. The student who accepts failure as feedback stays motivated to learn. The entrepreneur who builds from principle, not panic, stays the course. This is the balance Krishna champions: mental equilibrium, regardless of applause or adversity. This isn't detachment—it's a deeper form of engagement rooted in awareness.

Focus on Efforts, Not Just Outcomes

Chapter 2, Verse 47: "You have control over action alone, never its fruits. Do not let the fruits be your motive, but do not be attached to inaction."

This introduces a cornerstone principle: we are responsible for effort, not results. It urges us to act with full commitment but not be swayed by the outcome.

➤ *Play with purpose. The score will follow.*

By shifting our focus from results to effort, we free ourselves from unnecessary stress and disappointment. Growth comes not from controlling outcomes but from committing fully to the process. This principle fosters a mindset of resilience, reducing fear and sharpening clarity.

Entrepreneurs who embrace this philosophy find joy in building their vision, not just hitting milestones. It's a mindset that transforms how we approach a venture—**satisfaction lies in the journey, not just the destination.**

➤ *Inaction is a greater loss than failure.*

This verse also warns against inaction. Avoiding effort out of fear of failure or staying passive because the path is hard are subtle forms of self-sabotage. A product launch that flops may teach us more than the one that succeeds. Inaction creates stagnation.

Entrepreneurial Framework 2:

Seeing Through Illusion: Long-Term Value Over Hype

Entrepreneurs should focus on building valuable businesses and not get swayed by valuations and exit talks; exit opportunities with the right valuation will emerge at the right time.

Theme: Strategic clarity for sustainable growth, prioritizing long-term value over short-term hype.

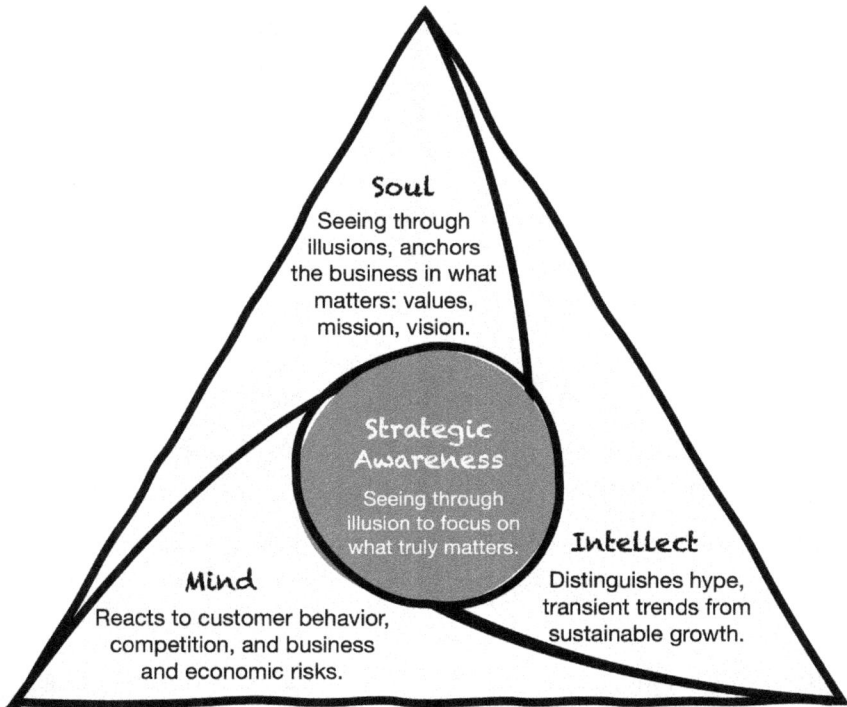

Soul
Seeing through illusions, anchors the business in what matters: values, mission, vision.

Strategic Awareness
Seeing through illusion to focus on what truly matters.

Intellect
Distinguishes hype, transient trends from sustainable growth.

Mind
Reacts to customer behavior, competition, and business and economic risks.

Business Insight:

Successful entrepreneurs train their minds to spot patterns in the market and use intellect to distinguish hype from the right opportunities. They sense market shifts and act on them before

35

anyone else, but they always stay anchored in their mission to avoid getting distracted by the noise of short-term trends. Those lured by quick wins of inflated valuations, media buzz, or fast exits may shine briefly but fail to endure.

Strategic clarity means making decisions rooted in your venture's True North to create long-term value. Anchor in purpose, not trends, to build a lasting impact. Pause, ask, *Does this opportunity strengthen our mission—or just looks good in the moment?*

➤ *A disciplined mind sees through illusions—and builds for what lasts.*

Discerning entrepreneurs consistently:

- Read market signals, not headlines
- Listen to real customer needs, not vanity metrics
- Build for resilience, not just recognition

In 2006, Mark Zuckerberg declined Yahoo's billion-dollar acquisition offer for two-year-old Facebook. At that fragile stage, the cash glittered like a fast track to success; instead, Mark saw a deeper pattern of user scale and its long-term impact over an early exit. That's strategic clarity in action.

Action Step: When hype calls, ask, "Does this align with my True North?" "Will this matter five years from now?" "Is this a signal or a shiny distraction?" Act on what aligns, not what impresses.

With **strategic clarity** in place, the next challenge is **executing with discipline**, which is explored in the next chapter.

Chapter 3
The Joy of Action

The third chapter of the *Gita* unfolds the fundamental Path of Action *(Karma Yoga)*. The discipline of righteous action with purpose, without being entangled in outcomes. When integrated into daily life, our duties become vehicles for growth, not weights we're forced to carry.

At its core, it is based on the universal law of balance—what we contribute through effort and value comes back to us as the impact we create, giving us deeper fulfillment. This isn't a transactional exchange. When our actions create true value for people and the planet, the ripple effects outlast fleeting applause.

This action mindset teaches us that true achievement is measured by the positive transformations of the lives we touch. When we dedicate ourselves to service and make meaningful contributions, whether in careers, relationships, or communities, success becomes a byproduct of the impact we create.

➤ *Sustained success is built on contribution, not control.*

This action mindset also tells us that inaction is detrimental to progress, as it disrupts the rhythm of growth. The universe operates in a state of constant change, and to stagnate is to fall behind. When we avoid responsibility, whether due to fear or hesitation, we interrupt the natural cycle of growth and progress.

In business, when indecision paralyzes action, it results in hidden costs, missed opportunities, eroded confidence, and lost momentum.

➤ *Responsibility, when avoided, leads to regret; when embraced, builds trust.*

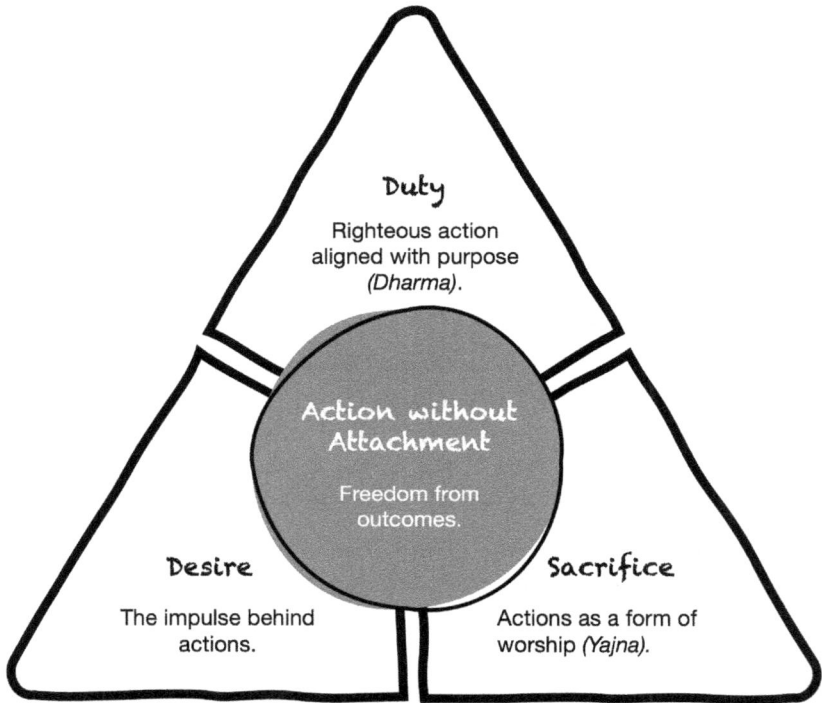

Bottom line: action is inevitable. We are all bound to it, and what matters is the intention. The key is a purpose-driven mindset, aiming for excellence over fleeting gains.

When we serve communities with sincerity, we find personal fulfillment. When our actions reflect our deeper values, life becomes less about outcomes and more about process. Work becomes less of a grind and more of a sacred rhythm. The reward is higher than success. It is the joy of fulfillment and a sense of direction that doesn't waver with external ups and downs.

This is the promise of the path of action: not perfection, but alignment; not fame, but fulfillment. When we lead from purpose, life flows not as a struggle for control but as a journey of harmony.

Lead by Example through Action

Chapter 3, Verse 26: "By abstaining from work, you will confuse the ignorant, who are engrossed in their actions."

This verse underscores our responsibility as influencers to lead by example. When we step back from action, it can mislead those that follow us.

Whether in business, politics, or social causes, people look up to those who lead. Leaders at every level must exemplify the principles they expect others to follow. If we shy away from responsibility or dodge our duty, it confuses and demotivates those we influence. A CEO who preaches innovation but avoids making difficult strategic decisions weakens the company's direction. A teacher who doesn't stay updated fails to inspire students.

➤ *Influence isn't what you preach—it's what you practice.*

This also extends to social and ethical responsibility. If we hold knowledge and resources yet do not act for the greater good of society, we reinforce a culture where personal goals trump collective success. When we stay engaged in righteous action, letting go of ego, we carve a path to guide and uplift others.

Beyond the Surface

Chapter 3, Verse 43: "Thus knowing yourself to be transcendental to material senses, mind and intelligence, O mighty-armed Arjun, you should not grieve."

We often define ourselves by what we achieve, what we own, or how we're perceived. This verse highlights the importance of understanding who we truly are beyond the material identities of status, titles, and wealth. Because when these measures of success are threatened or lost, our sense of identity shakes, causing stress, anxiety, and self-doubt.

Krishna reminds us that our essence is not found in these outer layers of identity. Beneath the roles, responsibilities, and expectations lies a constant—our inner identity. The one that experiences life but isn't swayed by its rollercoaster. This awareness of inner identity is practical wisdom that helps us hold success without clinging to it and to face setbacks without collapse.

▶ *You are not your outcomes—you are your awareness in action.*

When we tie our self-worth to job titles or performance, we struggle with insecurity when faced with challenges or career shifts. But when we cultivate an awareness of our deeper self-worth, we stop taking setbacks personally and start seeing each experience as information.

This mindset reduces overreactions and reframes failure. It's a shift from scarcity to abundance, from fear to trust, from control to clarity. Krishna's wisdom here is a quiet strength: when we see ourselves as more than our achievements or failures, we lead with calm, recover fast, grow with grace.

Entrepreneurial Framework 3:

Process over Prize

Entrepreneurs should find balance and harmony in work and life, detached from outcome, because the journey is a marathon and not a sprint.

Theme: Process fuels outcomes—stay committed to the process of building and iterating, and let your process deliver the prize.

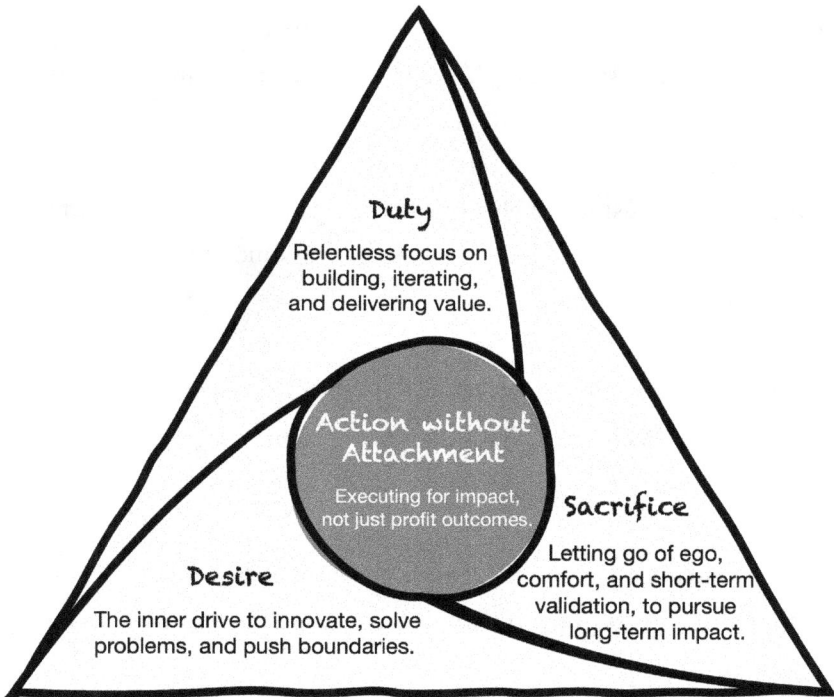

Business Insight:

Successful entrepreneurs pour their energy into the art of building, refining, and delivering, staying committed to the process, detached from the lure of shiny rewards. Execution shapes this path as we root our actions in duty, letting results bloom in their own time.

➤ *The best business builders don't chase applause—they chase alignment.*

The gleam of instant payoffs such as bonuses, headlines, applause, fades as fast as they flare. Instead, we must anchor every effort in our True North—and measure success by the value we create.

Pause, ask, *Does this task fuel our mission or just feeds our ego?*

Mastery isn't about ignoring outcomes but trusting our work to carve its own enduring mark, like a riverbed etched through years.

Howard Schultz shaped Starbucks into a "third place" for community, not just a coffee stop. It exemplifies execution with a vision, perfecting the experience, not chasing quick profits—a rhythm that built a legacy.

Action Step: When pressure rises, ask, "Am I focused on activities or progress?" "What is creating real value?" "Is it lasting value?" Return to the process—that's where excellence lives.

As **execution** becomes second nature, the next step is to integrate **wisdom and renunciation**, which is explored in the next chapter.

Chapter 4
The Power of Knowledge and Action

The fourth chapter of the *Gita*, ushers us into a deeper layer of insight where knowledge, action, and renunciation converge. Krishna elevates the conversation from merely doing to deeply understanding: **true action must be rooted in awareness.**

He introduces the idea that knowledge isn't just conceptual—it's also experiential. It's not about knowing more—it's about seeing more clearly. We rise above ignorance by gaining insight into the forces that shape our circumstances. When action is informed by insight and aligned with purpose, it becomes a vehicle for inner clarity, not just external accomplishment.

➤ *Wisdom isn't in knowing what to do—it's in knowing why it matters.*

We live in a world of high-speed environments. Without clarity, we risk reacting rather than leading, chasing momentum without direction. Krishna's guidance re-centers us: true success comes when knowledge and action work together—when we act with intention. That's when even ordinary tasks become instruments of transformation.

These universal principles are like stars in the night, guiding us through complexity and change. And for this knowledge to transform us, we must receive it with humility, sincerity, and faith. Because without that faith, we remain stuck in doubt—trapped in cycles of inaction, confusion, and untapped potential.

Krishna leads us to ask: *Are we driven by ego and applause, or are we building something meaningful?* By infusing our work with clarity and intention, we spark true progress for us and the world around us.

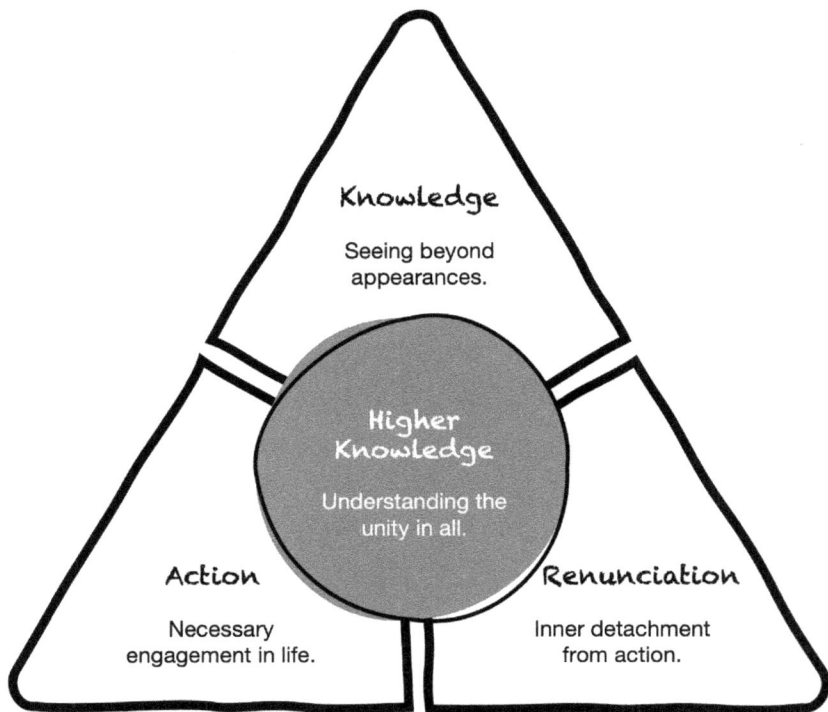

Knowledge
Seeing beyond appearances.

Higher Knowledge
Understanding the unity in all.

Action
Necessary engagement in life.

Renunciation
Inner detachment from action.

Another truth Krishna shares is the nuanced understanding of **inaction within action** and **action within inaction**. This paradox encourages us to look beyond appearances. Strategic pauses often produce the most decisive outcomes. And stillness becomes powerful amid chaos, allowing us to navigate challenges without losing our footing, to shatter inertia with intent clarity. This is the art of engaging fully without being consumed.

Krishna also lifts **faith and devotion** as guiding torches and essential drivers of growth. In a world dominated by skepticismthey keep us grounded in our commitment to the journey when outcomes aren't visible. Whether building a business, leading a team, or shaping a life, faith in the process builds resilience, and devotion gives us the confidence to overcome obstacles.

Another insight Krishna shares is the importance of mentorship, both in entrepreneurship and for personal evolution. Those who have walked farther can help us see more clearly when our vision blurs and we lose perspective. Knowledge alone doesn't transform. Only when it takes root in practice through proper guidance does it light the path forward.

▶ *Growth requires clarity, commitment, and a guide who helps you stay aligned.*

Krishna closes the chapter with an invitation: to use knowledge as a compass to rise above distractions. Because when action flows from understanding, we begin to move with direction and depth. Our efforts gain meaning. This is where real transformation begins.

Perceive the Inaction Within Action, and Vice Versa

Chapter 4, Verse 18: "One who sees inaction in action and action in inaction is wise among people. He is a yogi who has accomplished everything."

This is a very profound insight: a wise person sees the stillness in motion and motion in stillness. This means acting with inner calm even amidst intense activity. And that appearing still when lost in inner turmoil and hesitation is not true rest.

In our hyperactive world, where busyness is glorified, **we often mistake activity for progress**. Many hustle constantly, chasing outcomes without direction—that's activity without clarity. On the other hand, someone who pauses to reflect or reset may appear still—but if they're anchored in awareness, that pause is progress in motion.

▶ *Move with intention, not compulsion—pause with clarity, not confusion.*

A founder who slows down to realign a team's vision during a crisis may seem passive on the surface—but that reset can spark transformative momentum.

This message challenges us to look beyond appearances and ask, *What is the quality of our action? Are we moving from awareness or reacting from anxiety?*

When we master this balance of motion and stillness, our actions become purposeful. That's where efficiency meets effectiveness.

Cultivate Faith to Overcome Obstacles

Chapter 4, Verse 40: "The ignorant, the faithless, and the doubter perish. The man of faith succeeds."

Krishna asserts, without faith, growth is impossible. Faith fuels our pursuit of knowledge and action. Doubt, hesitation, and cynicism don't just choke growth, they stall our progress. Faith is not blind optimism, it is trusting the process when clarity is absent and results are slow to show.

Many promising ideas, ventures, and personal aspirations don't fail due to external obstacles—they crumble under internal doubt. An entrepreneur who wavers on their vision may abandon it at the first hurdle, while those who hold on with faith find ways through setbacks.

In our world of data and risk analysis, while faith may seem outdated, it remains essential. Because not every decision has a guaranteed outcome. Not every move will feel certain.

➤ *Faith is the bridge when logic ends and action must begin.*

A leader may be called to make a bold move without complete information. If they wait for perfect data, they miss the moment. In such moments, faith is the difference between bold momentum and prolonged hesitation.

Without faith in our principles or preparation, we freeze, delay, and retreat. But when faith is cultivated through experienced learning and reflection, it steadies us in uncertainty.

Faith is our bedrock of resilience—without faith, we remain stuck. With it, we move—imperfectly, perhaps, but forward. And in that motion, growth begins.

Entrepreneurial Framework 4:

Strategic Execution with Insight & the Power of Letting Go

Entrepreneurs should avoid distractions and temptations and exercise self-control to stay focused on the finish line.

Theme: Letting go of FOMO, resisting the temptation to chase every opportunity, and staying true to the core mission.

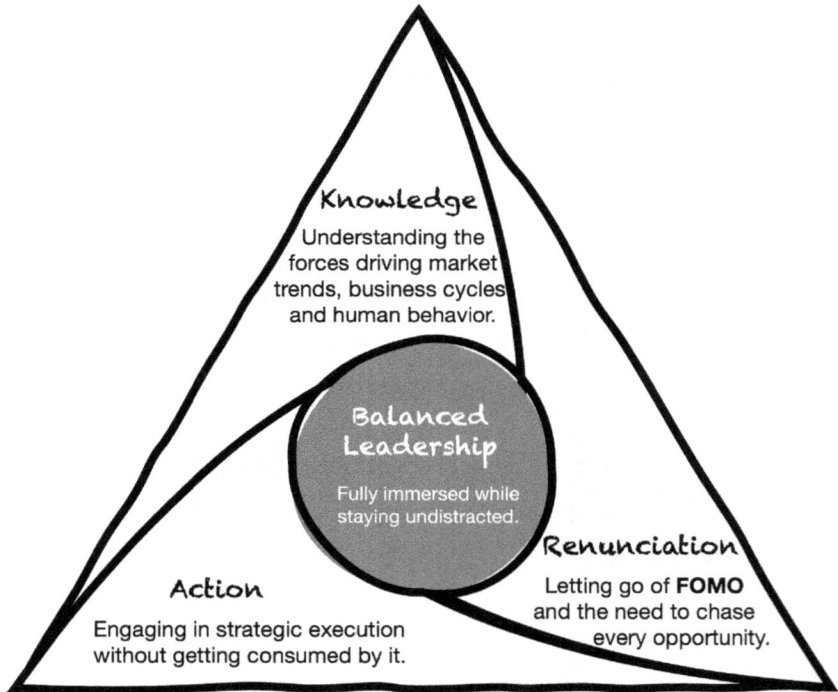

Knowledge
Understanding the forces driving market trends, business cycles and human behavior.

Balanced Leadership
Fully immersed while staying undistracted.

Renunciation
Letting go of **FOMO** and the need to chase every opportunity.

Action
Engaging in strategic execution without getting consumed by it.

Business Insight:

Great leaders combine knowledge with execution—balancing bold vision with hands-on action while renouncing distractions. In fast-moving markets, distractions are everywhere—trends, opportunities, and noise that tempt us away from our core mission. The most effective entrepreneurs are those who know **what not to pursue**.

➤ *Focus isn't just what you commit to—it's also what you consciously release.*

Effective entrepreneurs avoid the trap of chasing every trend out of FOMO (fear of missing out). They sharpen their focus on high-impact opportunities instead of spreading themselves too thin. The act on insights, not impulse.

The triad to practice: **action** grounded in purpose, **knowledge** that informs strategy, and **renunciation** of distractions that dilute impact.

Warren Buffett's success stems from his ability to *know* what drives value, *act* with disciplined conviction, and *renounce* the noise of short-term market hype.

Action Step: When options multiply, pause to ask, "What do signals reveal?" "What serves the mission?" "Is it a distraction?" Cut distractions, act with clarity.

With **knowledge guiding action**, the next step is to **balance renunciation and action**, which is explored in the next chapter.

Chapter 5
Freedom Through Renunciation

The fifth chapter of the *Gita*, reframes renunciation (*Sannyasa*) not as withdrawal from the world, but as the release of pride from outcomes.

True renunciation is about letting go of the inner need to control, or the ego, to be obsessed by outcomes. It is not outer withdrawal but **inner detachment** that frees us from cycles of expectation, disappointment, and suffering. Krishna calls us to perform every action selflessly and let the outcomes manifest naturally, free from the mental burden of control.

We often connect wealth, praise, recognition, and success to "me" and "mine" only to find stress shadowing our gains and losses. Krishna urges us to shift our focus from WHAT we gain (outcomes) to WHY we act (purpose). Renouncing the sense of "me" and "mine" and seeing actions as offerings for a higher purpose. It is then that fulfillment flows, and we rise to resilience and peace. Ego fades, purpose holds. This teaching is both radical and refreshing.

➤ *When ego steps aside, purpose takes the lead.*

The root cause of suffering is not in action but attachment to its results. We suffer when expectations are unmet, when recognition doesn't come, or when outcomes don't match our effort. By offering our actions to a higher purpose, without clinging to returns, we reclaim our peace and inner stability.

In business, renunciation doesn't mean being indifferent to results—it's about staying grounded in purpose, even when outcomes fluctuate. Leaders who operate from this space make wiser decisions, carry less stress, and foster more trust. They act with commitment, not control.

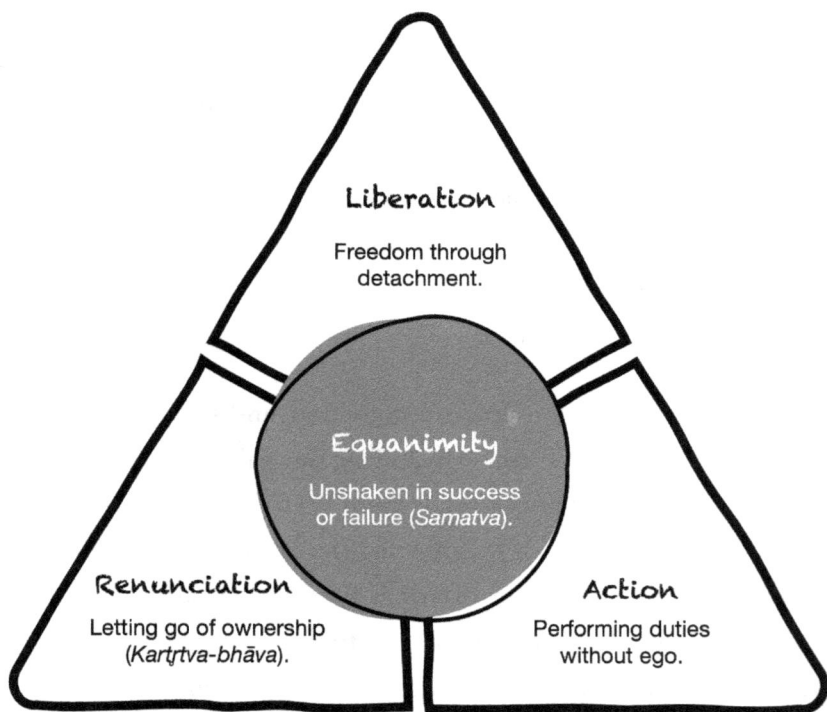

Krishna also distinguishes between equanimity through selfless action, where we act with detachment, and equanimity through renunciation, where we act without ego. In the latter, there is no "me" or "mine" entangled in success or failure—there is only the presence in the action.

For business leaders, this distinction this reflects in how they make decisions and lead teams. Selfless action enables them to make tough calls with composure. Renunciation takes it further: they lead with team spirit, without clinging to personal credit or blame. They take ownership of the mission but don't let success inflate their pride or failure undermine their identity.

➤ *Renunciation isn't retreat—it's refinement, an inner shift.*

When we relinquish ownership of outcomes and act from purpose, we stop reacting to life and begin responding with clarity, calm, and conviction.

Renunciation Leads to Self-Realization

Chapter 5, Verse 6: "Renunciation is difficult without yoga practice. The sage engaged in yoga soon attains Brahman."

Renunciation is not easy—it requires preparation and consistent practice. Letting go of the ego's grip doesn't happen overnight, and it is tough without *Yoga's* discipline. *Yoga*, in this context, is not physical postures but the alignment of mind, body, and spirit—training us to rise above attachment with every breath.

This means cultivating habits and mindsets that align action with purpose—practices that center us when the ego wants to take over. *Yoga* becomes the practice for inner alignment: to act with awareness, not impulse. Without the foundation of this discipline, renunciation can become forced or superficial.

➤ *Discipline is focused surrender—presence without attachment.*

This teaching is highly relevant in moments of uncertainty or emotional overload. A leader may have to make a tough call without taking credit. A professional might need to do the right thing, even when it goes unnoticed. This is where practice matters—because the ego's pull is strong, and without practice, renunciation turns into avoidance or frustration.

This speaks of emotional mastery with a twist. When we blend action with inner stillness, we are fully present yet unbound. This mindfulness brings a sense of peace, and we engage with clarity and authenticity.

Overcome Destructive Impulses to Find Happiness

Chapter 5, Verse 23: "One who is able to withstand here on earth the impulse of desire and anger before giving up the body is a yogi and a happy person."

Krishna points to two major forces that disturb our peace and cloud our judgement: desire and anger. Both are natural, modern life constantly fuels these impulses. Desire shows up as ambition without reflection, consumption without restraint, or constant comparison. Anger emerges when our expectations are unmet or when control is threatened. Krishna doesn't condemn these feelings—but he warns against letting them take over, because they can derail judgment, relationships, and clarity.

➤ *You don't need to suppress emotion—but you do need to steer it.*

In leadership, emotional regulation is non-negotiable. A leader who reacts in anger breaks trust. One who chases every opportunity out of desire loses focus. But a leader who pauses, reflects, and chooses their response earns credibility and influence.

In personal life, too, moments of anger can fracture relationships or lead to decisions we later regret. But when we cultivate restraint and learn to pause, reflect, and respond without being ruled by it, we unlock peace and power.

It also applies to consumerism and pleasure hunting—both marketed as happiness. If unchecked, they spiral into a craving's trap.

Krishna's message is clear: happiness isn't found in satisfying every impulse but in freedom from being enslaved by them. It is found in mastery over our mind.

Entrepreneurial Framework 5:

Empowered Leadership: Clarity, Focus and Delegation

An entrepreneur should recognize the importance of proper understanding of the context and situations to avoid making impulsive and uninformed decisions.

Theme: Letting go of micromanagement and trusting teams to execute while focusing on the bigger picture.

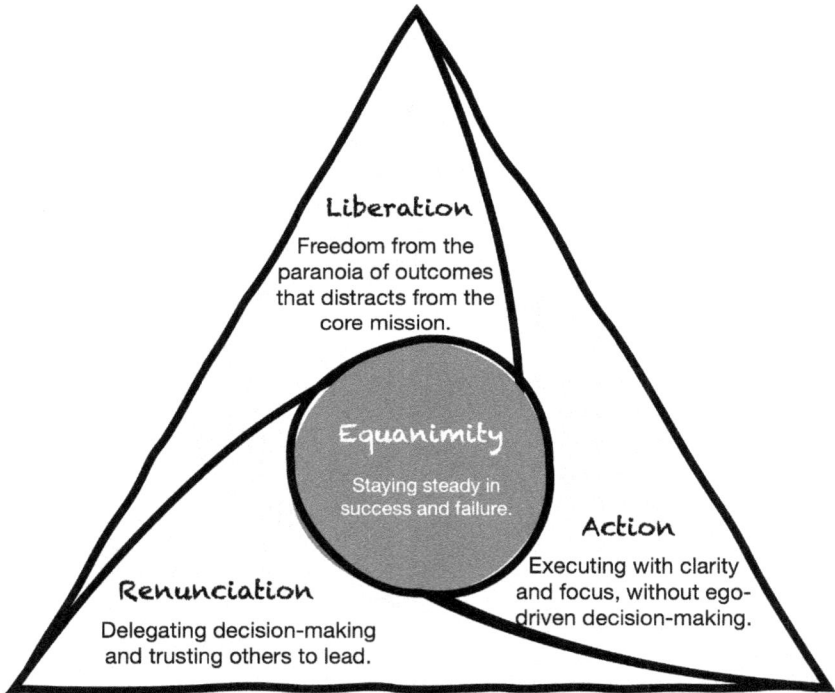

Business Insight:

One of the biggest challenges founders face is the desire to control every detail. This impulse often stems from fear—fear of failure, fear of trusting others, or fear of losing their own relevance. But enduring leadership isn't about doing everything. It is about doing what matters most and empowering others to own the rest.

➤ *Letting go is not a weakness—it's a strategy.*

Micromanagement is common in early-stage ventures when the business feels deeply personal. But as the company grows, so must the mindset of the leader. Great leaders **set direction, invest in their teams**, and then **step back**—not to disengage, but to let people rise.

This is where inner detachment (renunciation) becomes a leadership superpower. By letting go of the need for constant control or personal credit, founders create space for teams to perform, make decisions, and take ownership.

This mindset fosters a culture of ownership and innovation: teams rise, take charge, and solve problems creatively. By releasing the need to control, leaders create space for creativity and growth. They build organizations that thrive not just on their efforts but on the collective strength of their people.

Reed Hastings, Netflix, exemplifies this culture of freedom and responsibility. His leadership focused on clarity of vision—not control—enabling talented people to make decisions without layers of approval.

Action Step: When stakes rise, ask, "Should I own or delegate?" "Needs my attention or my trust?" "Who can do this better?" Empower others, scale with trust.

With **renunciation and action** balanced, the next step is to **cultivate deep focus**, which is explored in the next chapter.

Chapter 6
Mastery of the Mind

The sixth chapter of the *Gita*, leads us to inner transformation through the path of meditation (*Dhyana*). Krishna introduces meditation not as an escape from the world but as a discipline of stillness, the strength of presence, a path to mastery of the mind, and realizing the self.

Through sustained focus and mental stillness, we experience inner alignment. When we recognize the eternal self —the part of us beyond the body, mind, and senses, the self that is not swayed by outcomes, emotions, or the highs and lows of the world. That's when true enlightenment occurs.

▶ *Mastery of the mind to know the eternal self is mastery of life.*

To rise above the material distractions, Krishna urges us to understand the influence of the three energies that manifest as qualities, or *Gunas*. *Sattva* brings purity and perfection, *Rajas* creates ambition and desire, and *Tamas* produces inertia and ignorance. These forces shape how we think, feel, and act. Meditation helps us observe these forces and rise above their sway.

Krishna emphasizes meditation as a way of life, not an isolated practice. Through meditation we can experience inner peace. We free ourselves from mental agitation, unchecked desires, and the turmoil from external chaos and unify with the universal energy that flows within and around us.

► *You don't need to eliminate distraction—you need to rise above it with discipline.*

The mastery of the mind through meditation yields tangible results: sharper decisions, deeper empathy, steadier emotions, clarity under pressure, better relationships, and overall well-being. It trains us to witness thoughts and emotions without judgment, thus responding to conflicts with patience and empathy.

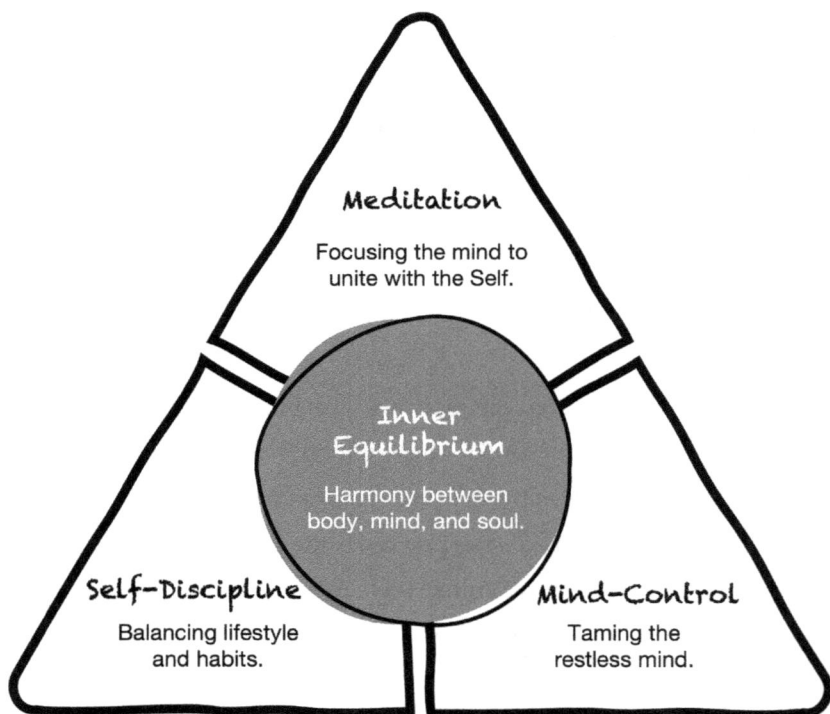

Meditation
Focusing the mind to unite with the Self.

Inner Equilibrium
Harmony between body, mind, and soul.

Self-Discipline
Balancing lifestyle and habits.

Mind-Control
Taming the restless mind.

By grasping the play of the *Gunas*, we notice our own patterns. Leaders who recognize when they are being pulled by *Rajas,* chasing growth without reflection, or *Tamas,* resisting difficult decisions, can course-correct and re-center. They also keep *Sattva* grounded to stop it from drifting into perfectionism.

Krishna presents meditation as the supreme path to transformation—one that integrates discipline, devotion, and self-awareness for sustained excellence. When we master our minds, we elevate every dimension of our lives, from business and work to love and creativity. We shift from reaction to reflection, from distraction to direction. Everything else begins to align.

Moderation and Discipline Reduce Suffering

Chapter 6, Verse 17: "For the yogi who is moderate in eating, recreation, working, sleeping, and waking, yoga destroys all sorrow."

Krishna champions balance because both indulgence and austerity breed suffering. Moderation leads to stability and well-being. *Yogic* discipline doesn't mean suppression—it invites rhythm. He urges us to adopt moderation in all areas of life: food, rest, work, and play. When you maintain harmony in life's rhythm—physical, mental, and spiritual—the mind steadies, making space for higher awareness.

In modern life, imbalance creeps in unnoticed. Overwork leads to burnout. Overindulgence leads to guilt or fatigue. Distraction fragments attention. Skipped sleep erodes vitality. Krishna's guidance is simple: measured moderation—not excess or denial—is the key to sustainable success. Mindful work, intentional rest, and purposeful recreation nurture energy that lasts.

➤ *Discipline isn't restriction—it's a design for sustained flow.*

Leaders who live by this principle build healthier work cultures—where push is paired with pause and performance is balanced by recovery. Professionals who harmonize work and well-being don't just avoid burnout—they spark creativity and efficiency. Such a rhythmic balance not only boosts productivity—it builds resilience.

Krishna reminds us that suffering doesn't always come from hardship—it often stems from imbalance. By practicing moderation, we preserve our energy to navigate life's challenges with resilience.

Meditation: The Supreme Path to Transformation

Chapter 6, Verse 46: "The yogi is superior to those performing austerities, and superior to the wise, and even superior to the doers of meritorious deeds."

Krishna elevates meditation above all other paths—not to dismiss them, but to underscore that **inner stillness enables everything else to work better.**

In a world driven by activity, silence can feel unfamiliar or even uncomfortable. Yet it is in silence that awareness deepens. When we learn to sit with thoughts without judgment, without being pulled by them, clarity, creativity, and compassion emerge.

➤ *Breakthroughs happen when the noise fades and awareness takes over.*

Many of the world's top innovators find breakthroughs in stillness, not rush. By quieting the mind, we tap into intuition and clarity that enhance problem-solving and decision-making.

➤ *Stillness becomes a strategy. Reflection becomes fuel.*

The meditative mind teaches us to pause before reacting, to listen more deeply, and to stay grounded in moments of pressure. It strengthens emotional intelligence—enabling us to lead with calm, connect with empathy, and respond with care. When we cultivate inner stillness, we gain outer clarity. And from that clarity, right action becomes easier to see—and easier to take.

Entrepreneurial Framework 6:

Focused Leadership: Discipline & Strategy

True entrepreneurial innovation demands inner wisdom through disciplined focus, without losing sight of the larger purpose or vision.

Theme: Mastering focus by eliminating distractions to create space for deep strategic thinking and innovation.

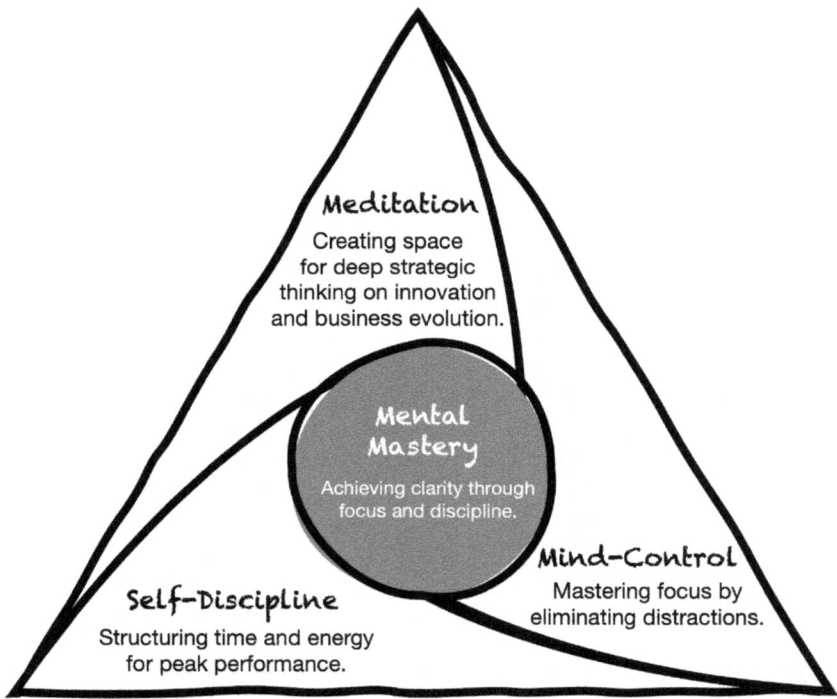

Meditation
Creating space for deep strategic thinking on innovation and business evolution.

Mental Mastery
Achieving clarity through focus and discipline.

Mind-Control
Mastering focus by eliminating distractions.

Self-Discipline
Structuring time and energy for peak performance.

Business Insight:

Startup founders are constantly bombarded with distractions—emails, meetings, market shifts, and investor pressures. This isn't just about execution—it's about foreseeing industry shifts, exploring new markets, innovating business models, and staying ahead of the curve. In this environment, the biggest competitive advantage isn't speed. It's **focus**.

▶ *In a distracted world, focus is a superpower.*

Founders disciplined to carve out space for deep thinking gain a competitive edge by making thoughtful, high-impact decisions that others miss in the noise.

Focused leadership is about structure. It's about managing time, attention, and mental energy like a limited resource. This isn't about doing less—it's about doing **what matters most** with full presence.

Bill Gates' famous "Think Weeks," where he isolated himself to read and reflect, exemplify the power of deep focus in driving innovation.

Action Step: When noise rises, ask, "Can I still my mind?" "Is this a reaction or a reflection?" "Should I pause to ponder?" They lead with calm and clarity.

With **deep focus and mental mastery** established, the next step is to **deepen insights and strategic knowledge**, which is explored in the next chapter.

Chapter 7
Lifting the Veil of Illusion

The seventh chapter of the *Gita* introduces *Vijnana* the applied dimension of wisdom. Where knowledge (*Jnana*) reveals truth, its application (*Vijnana*) makes it usable. From knowing to experiencing the truth is the path from realization to transformation.

It's not enough to grasp principles—what matters is whether they reshape how we think, act, and evolve. Just as science moves from hypothesis to application, wisdom must move from insight to embodiment. This is the transition from knowing to becoming.

Krishna begins to unravel the deeper layers of how the world truly works. He speaks of *Maya*, a layered illusion that distorts perception and binds us to short-term desires, external identities, and misplaced priorities. This illusion keeps us chasing outcomes, unaware that we've become reactive to the surface rather than anchored in the deeper flow of life.

It traps us both through fear, pain, or loss and through pleasure, gain, and attachment. It seduces us with the illusion that success will last forever and deceives us into believing that failure is the end of the road. Whether through the dread of endings or the highs of winning, this illusion disturbs our equilibrium—making us reactive rather than rooted in inner stillness.

➤ *Wisdom begins when illusion is recognized and seen clearly for what it is.*

Krishna explains that this illusion operates through the three energies that govern our inner lens. When we mistake intensity for progress, we're under the spell of *Rajas*. When we choose comfort over clarity, *Tamas* has the reins. When we align action with awareness, *Sattva* emerges—not as a virtue, but as a natural result of inner coherence. These forces shape our experiences: moods, decisions, behaviors, and even our worldview.

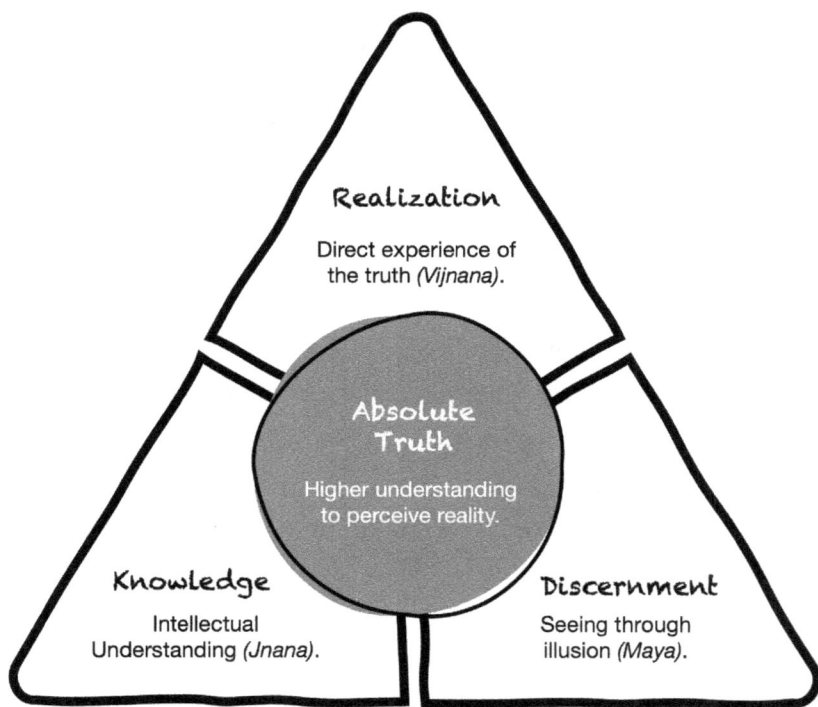

▶ *Clarity means nothing until it guides how we live, choose, and lead.*

The illusion of *Maya* is glamour without depth, momentum without meaning, and growth without purpose. We strive hard, but toward what end? Knowledge helps us recognize this pattern, but only its application helps us exit it. That's the real liberation—living with experience, not just thinking about it.

The teaching is clear: stop intellectualizing truth and start operationalizing it—that's how wisdom becomes a lived force. That's the way to pierce the veil of illusion to reveal what's real—it reshapes how we show up, decide, and lead.

The Transformative Energy in Nature

Chapter 7, Verse 4: "Earth, water, fire, air, ether, mind, intellect, and ego—these are the eightfold division of My nature."

Krishna explains that his material energy expresses itself through five elements of nature (earth, water, fire, air, and ether/space) and three inner faculties (mind, intellect, and ego). Together they form the field of material nature (*Prakriti*). This verse reframes our environment as a sacred expression infused with universal energy and divine intelligence.

This shift elevates how we relate to the world around us. Feeling the earth beneath our feet, the warmth of the sun, the glow of the moon, the flow of water, and the breath of the wind—these aren't just sensory experiences; these are moments that connect us to something bigger. When we connect with nature, we derive transformative energy from it.

➤ *Connection with nature isn't sensory rhetoric—it's strategic alignment with the energy that sustains us.*

Step into a forest, surrounded by towering trees and the soothing melody of birdsong. Or feel the gentle breeze rustling through your hair. These aren't just breaks; they energize and rejuvenate us, lower our stress, and clear our heads. They return us to the source we often forget we're part of.

Including mind, intellect, and ego in this mix shows our inner world is tied to the outer one. The same intelligence animates both. Aligning with that truth, we tap into its strength, find peace inside, and bond with the outside. Krishna's words make it simple: **nature doesn't just surround us—its energy transforms us when we allow it to.**

Transcending Illusions to Overcome Limitations

Chapter 7, Verse 14: "Those who take refuge in Me can cross over this illusion of death."

This verse isn't about physical mortality—it speaks to the cyclical nature of existence. The illusion of *Maya* instills fear of endings: fear of loss, separation, and scarcity. But what appears to end is simply transitioning. The end of a role, a venture, or a phase of life may seem like a loss, but it's often the beginning of reinvention and rediscovery.

▶ *Illusion tells us we're stuck. Wisdom reminds us we're evolving.*

The transition through cycles of transformation in business, work, or relationships meets with resistance to change. It is the illusion of *Maya* that makes us cling to models, identities, or bonds that no longer serve us. We fear letting go because we mistake the form for the essence. But Krishna reframes change not as destruction but as movement. With this clarity, we cease to see setbacks and transitions as losses and begin to experience them as necessary evolution.

This insight is vital for entrepreneurs and leaders. Innovation requires moving past outdated structures. Adaptation means leaving familiar comfort zones. Transformation requires faith—what's ahead is not a threat but expansion.

Maya clouds us with limits of security and loss. We hesitate to take risks—whether switching careers, launching a new business, or making bold life choices. But nothing is ever lost. Change is constant. The way forward is with courage and clarity, not caution or delusion.

Krishna's message is unmistakable: **see beyond the illusion of endings, and all limits fall away.**

Entrepreneurial Framework 7:

Validated Wisdom: Strategy, Insights & Execution

An entrepreneur should cultivate both strategic knowledge and deep market insights to navigate complex landscapes in which their businesses operate.

Theme: From insight to embodiment, from noticing market signals to real-world validation, becoming aligned is what truly matters. (*Signal→Validation→Alignment*)

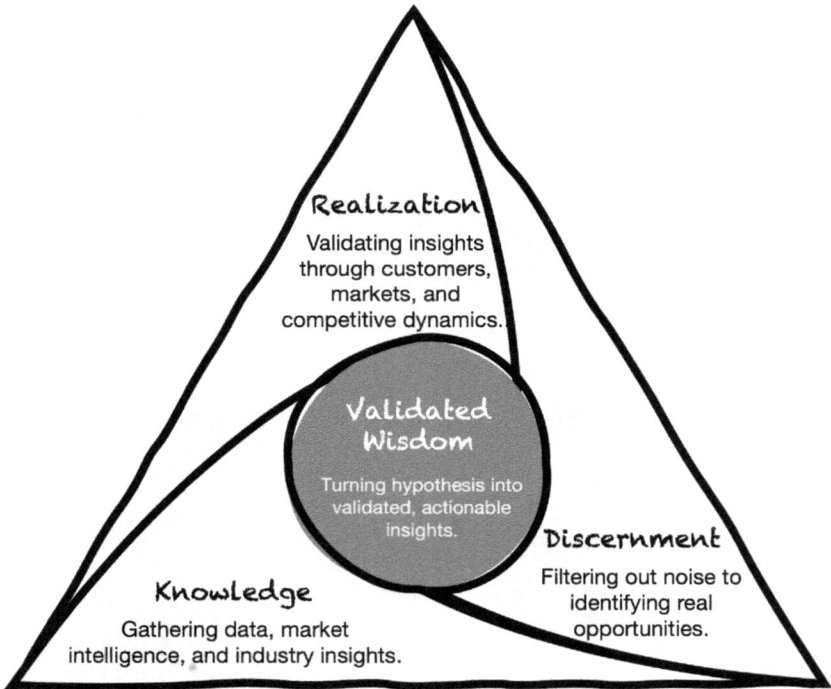

Realization
Validating insights through customers, markets, and competitive dynamics.

Validated Wisdom
Turning hypothesis into validated, actionable insights.

Discernment
Filtering out noise to identifying real opportunities.

Knowledge
Gathering data, market intelligence, and industry insights.

Business Insight:

In business, and more importantly in the startup world, knowledge is abundant—but clarity is rare. Knowledge alone isn't enough—it must be validated in the real world. Founders need market intelligence, competitor analysis, and strategic insights, but their real edge comes from discernment: knowing what matters, what's a distraction, and what's worth acting on. But discernment alone isn't enough. Insights must be validated by customers, tested in the competitive space, and turned into actionable strategies.

▶ *Insight without validation is noise. Wisdom emerges through action.*

The entrepreneurs who move from "knowing" to "executing with clarity" become wiser with every cycle—not because they know more, but because they act on what's real. Wisdom isn't conceptual—it's validated through action.

Netflix's shift from DVD rentals to streaming was driven by deep insights into changing consumer behavior and technological trends.

Action Step: When it feels uncertain, pause to ask, "Can I test this?" "Is it a transition?" "Should I restart?" Observe, listen, test, and execute.

With **validated wisdom**, the next step is to align with **long-term vision and sustainability**, which are explored in the next chapter.

Chapter 8
Breaking Free from the Cycle

The eighth chapter of the *Gita* explores the universal consciousness that pervades everything. Krishna calls it *Brahman*—the eternal, unchanging reality that lies beneath all forms and experiences. This reorients how we view change, endings, and our place in the world.

He explains that real enlightenment comes from seeing the universal consciousness as timeless. It flows through all that exists, untouched by the rise and fall of external situations. When we root ourselves in what is permanent, we stop clinging to what is temporary.

➤ *True stability isn't control over change—it's clarity through change.*

This chapter touches on death and rebirth as metaphors for transitions. Life events such as the loss of a loved one, a breakup, an accident, or illness are inflection points that usher us into a new phase of being. Krishna teaches that our final thoughts shape what comes next. What we dwell on becomes our trajectory. The choices we make, the attention we give, the bonds we build, and the values we live by—these are not just personal habits or actions; they are future-shaping forces.

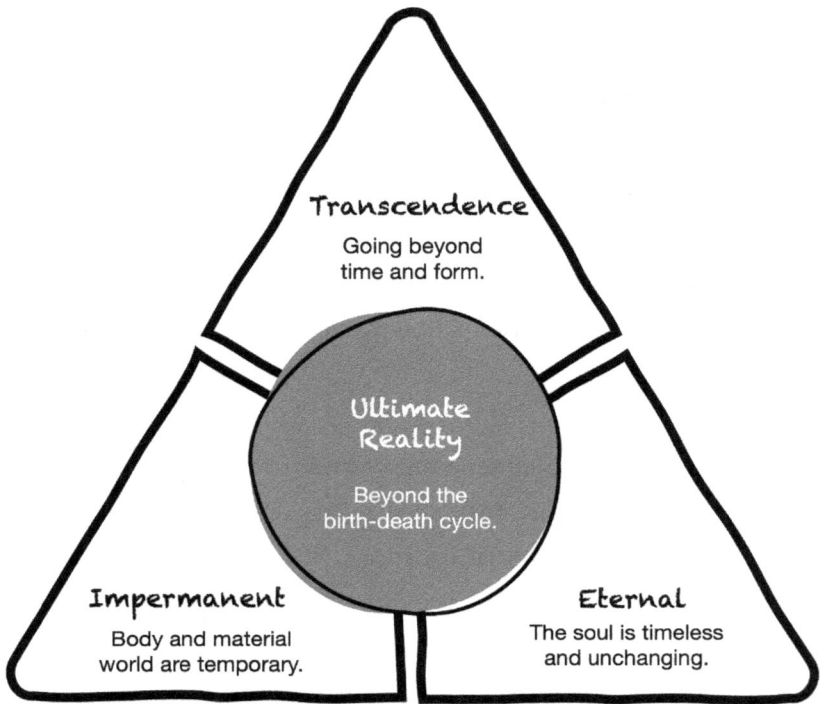

Transcendence
Going beyond
time and form.

Ultimate
Reality

Beyond the
birth-death cycle.

Impermanent
Body and material
world are temporary.

Eternal
The soul is timeless
and unchanging.

Knowing that life is temporary strips away distraction and brings us back to what actually matters: the purpose. Death, in this context, is not an end but a transition point. That shift in perspective encourages renewal, not fear.

In personal life, we move through phases—childhood to youth, youth to adulthood, adulthood to parenthood, parenthood to empty nest, and eventually to elderhood. Each phase brings a transition. What we carry forward—our experiences, relationships, and character—shapes the next. Our awareness in the present is not separate from our direction in the future. Our thoughts and intentions that guide our actions today also carve our ultimate destiny.

In business, this principle mirrors the importance of innovation and reinvention. Embracing the transition and letting go of outdated technologies or business models isn't a loss—it creates space for new cycles of growth. Those who resist change remain stuck; those who embrace it evolve.

▶ *Endings are not exits—they're invitations to the next cycle of creation.*

Krishna says that among the different paths to liberation—through devotion, knowledge, or action—the **method matters less than the mindset.** What truly defines our path is **intention**: what we value, what we aim for, and what we can let go of in order to grow.

The pursuit of *Brahman*, the universal consciousness, can be seen as a pursuit of deeper meaning in any area of life. Whether it's building a company, nurturing a relationship, or finding fulfillment in solitude, clarity of intention makes the process purposeful.

To summarize, *Brahman* is the imperishable consciousness, the unchanging reality beneath all change. Our actions and awareness in this life shape the journey beyond it. The values, culture, and lessons we build in one phase of business or leadership carry forward into the next pivot, the next venture, and the next chapter. What endures like the *Brahman* is not the form but the essence: clarity of vision, strength of culture, and the karma of contribution. When anchored in this deeper awareness we evolve shaping each new cycle with the wisdom of the last.

Total Dedication Leads to Success

Chapter 8, Verse 14: "Focus your mind on Me, be devoted to Me, worship Me, bow down to Me—then you shall come to Me."

Krishna emphasizes that undivided attention is essential for higher realization. In the spiritual context, it is devotion. In daily life, it is the full commitment required for transformation—a single-minded focus on what truly matters. Whether it's career excellence, deepening relationships, or mastering a craft, when we channel our energy with purpose and consistency, extraordinary outcomes follow.

In today's hyper-distracted world, it's easy to drift from our long-term vision and goals. When we stay focused on a mission, a principle, or a calling—and give it all we've got—it creates a powerful momentum. Those who are half-in, half-out rarely go far.

➤ *Thought without commitment is just potential. Commitment turns it into progress.*

Entrepreneurs who remain loyal to their vision—even while adapting to change—build resilient ventures. Professionals who continuously refine their skills, instead of chasing every trend, build expertise that compounds. Relationships deepen and flourish when nurtured with full presence, not fragmented attention.

Krishna's invitation is clear: where your attention goes, your life follows. Total dedication to bringing alignment between action, intent, and purpose drives success.

Shaping the Next Evolution Through Awareness

Chapter 8, Verse 24: "Fire, light, daytime, the bright fortnight, the six months of the northern solstice—departing by these, the knowers of Brahman go to Brahman."

This verse uses the symbolism of natural cycles of fire, light, day, the moon's phase, and the solstice to illustrate how transitions shape trajectories. Just as these luminous moments mark auspicious shifts in nature, Krishna teaches that our state of consciousness during transitions—whether daily, at inflection points, or between life phases—determines what unfolds next.

In business and leadership, the parallel is striking. How we exit a role, wrap up a project, or close a chapter sets the tone for what follows. If we leave with frustration, resentment, or unresolved issues, that energy often carries forward. But when we transition with learning, gratitude, and grace, we create space for the next evolution and growth to unfold with clarity. The mindset we exit with becomes the momentum we carry into the next cycle.

▶ *The way we end things shapes the way we begin again.*

Entrepreneurs who reflect on failed experiments evolve faster. Those who avoid reflection remain trapped in loops of uncertainty and repetition. The same is true with life: our growth through transition is shaped by how we resolve challenges. When we learn, adapt, and act, we rise. When we resist change, we find ourselves in a time trap.

This principle also applies to innovation. Some businesses wind down strategies or products under pressure or panic. Others step back with foresight, intention, and purpose—they are the ones best prepared to seize new opportunities. When we embrace transition intentionally, rather than resist it, we evolve instead of circling the same patterns.

Krishna's point is not about celestial timing—it's about inner timing. Our trajectory through change is shaped less by the change itself and more by how consciously we move through it. When we are awake to what is unfolding, we rise above the illusion of endings and cross into the next phase with momentum—not baggage.

Entrepreneurial Framework 8:

Enduring Impact: Long-Term Vision & Strategic Resilience

When markets shift and strategies rebound, it's not disruption—it's an invitation to realign, renew, and evolve through change with purpose.

Theme: Driving long-term vision in business requires adapting to changes in the market cycle while staying rooted in core values.

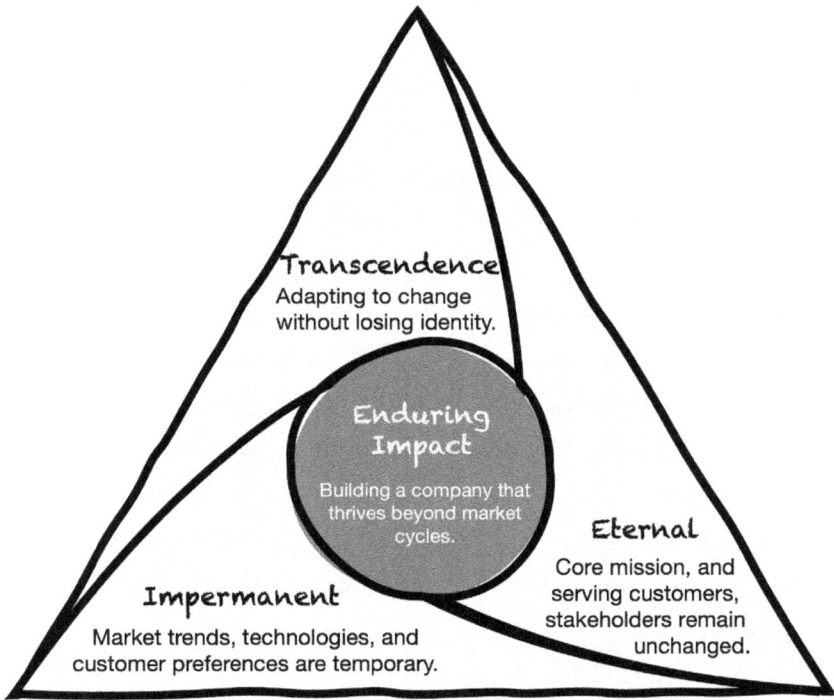

Transcendence
Adapting to change without losing identity.

Enduring Impact
Building a company that thrives beyond market cycles.

Eternal
Core mission, and serving customers, stakeholders remain unchanged.

Impermanent
Market trends, technologies, and customer preferences are temporary.

Business Insight:

Many startups fail because they over-index on fleeting trends without building a durable core. The most successful founders understand a deeper truth: the future belongs to those who balance

adaptability (responding to change with clarity) and **stability** (staying anchored in core values).

➤ *Adapt what's tactical. Protect what's timeless.*

Every business cycle presents two kinds of change:

- **Cyclical change** requires patience. It comes and goes.
- **Structural change** demands transformation. It resets the rules.

Great entrepreneurs know how to read both—and act accordingly. They know how to master the balance between what must evolve—products, strategies, and markets—and what must remain unchanged—vision, values, and principles.

Apple has reinvented itself through multiple waves of technology—personal computing, mobile devices, services—yet its core commitment to simplicity, design, and seamless user experience has never changed. That's not just innovation, it's anchored evolution.

Action Step: When change hits, leaders ask, "What bends, what holds?" "Cyclical or Structural?" "Persevere or Pivot?" They adapt smart, build big.

With a **long-term vision** in place, the next step is to uncover **hidden market insights**, which is explored in the next chapter.

Chapter 9
Fulfillment Through Commitment

The ninth chapter of the *Gita*, presents devotion (*Bhakti*) as the most direct and fulfilling path to realize higher truth. Krishna introduces devotion not as ritual but as heartfelt commitment to something greater than oneself. Unlike other yogic paths that emphasize knowledge or discipline, the path of devotion is accessible to all. It's not bound by status, intellect, or tradition—it flows from sincerity.

Krishna reveals that this is transformational; it bypasses complexity by aligning the heart and the will. When we commit to a purpose with love and trust, the journey itself becomes meaningful. The practice doesn't rely on perfection—it's built on consistency, humility, and depth of intention.

➤ *Commitment rooted in love is more powerful than mastery rooted in ego.*

At work and in business, it is the devotion to our craft, mission, or team. It becomes the energy that fuels purposeful creation—not because we're chasing praise or profits, but because we care deeply about the impact. Strategy, systems, and skills still matter, but devotion brings them to life. It turns work into worship.

In relationships, devotion becomes the practice of offering oneself consistently and generously, without expectations. It's love that isn't conditional on outcome. The artist who loses himself in the work, the founder who finds meaning in the build, the mentor who serves without a scoreboard—each lives this principle in action.

When we bring this kind of devoted sincerity into our actions, everything gains a deeper resonance. Work becomes more than achievement. Relationships become more than exchange. Creativity becomes more than performance. They all become expressions of something deeply meaningful, personal, and transcendent.

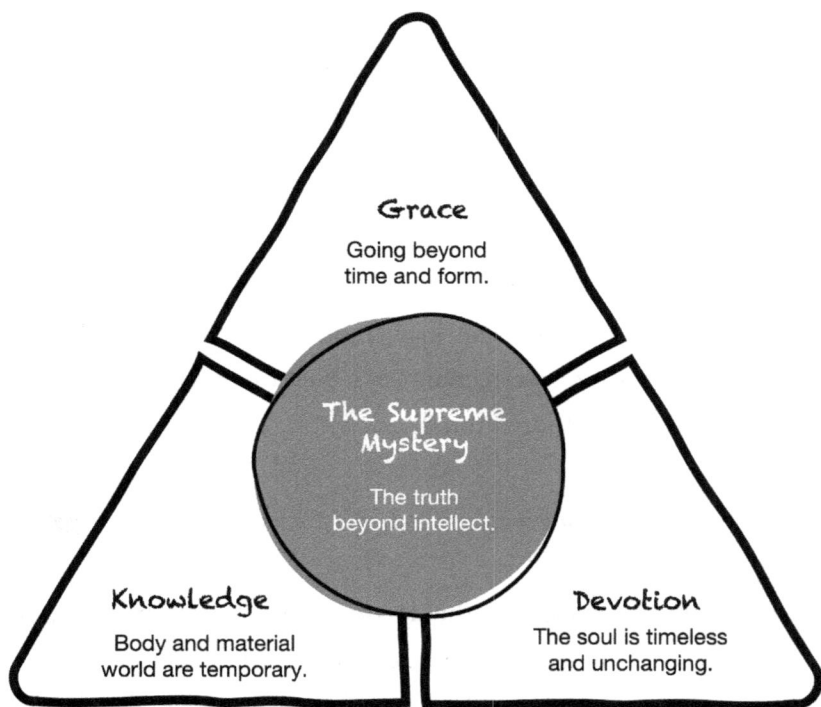

Grace
Going beyond time and form.

The Supreme Mystery
The truth beyond intellect.

Knowledge
Body and material world are temporary.

Devotion
The soul is timeless and unchanging.

Krishna also makes clear that true devotion is not confined by cultural rituals or societal norms—what matters most is the authenticity of our intent, genuine love, care, and connection from the heart. When we act with this mindset, we create deeper bonds and a more meaningful life—turning even simple actions into offerings. Work now stops being a grind, relationships grow beyond transactions, and creation feels like a gift. Through this devotion, we transcend mediocrity and step into fulfillment.

Dedication Unlocks Higher Understanding

Chapter 9, Verses 2 & 22: "This supreme knowledge isn't for scholars. Easy to grasp, pure, and joyful, it can be attained only through unswerving devotion."

Krishna emphasizes that the highest knowledge isn't reserved for the intellectual elite—it is revealed through wholehearted commitment. This verse reminds us that **deep understanding grows through love for the work, not just analysis of it**.

➤ *When the heart commits, the mind opens.*

This is a powerful leadership and learning principle: you don't master something by dissecting it alone, but by immersing yourself in it. Whether it's building a company, leading a team, raising a family, or pursuing personal development—real progress comes when you commit with heart and consistency.

Entrepreneurs who pour themselves into solving a real problem often find breakthroughs where others see dead ends. Leaders who genuinely care about their teams inspire a trust that no strategy slide can replicate. Artists who create from a place of love—not just for acclaim—produce work that resonates more deeply. Professionals who commit to learning—not just for credentials but for craft—unlock understanding that sticks.

Krishna's teaching is clear: when we bring love and loyalty to the path we're walking, the road begins to reveal itself.

Sincere Intentions Over Grand Gestures

Chapter 9, Verse 26: "Whoever offers a leaf, a flower, a fruit, or water with sincerity, I accept that offering."

This is the essence of devotion: a small act, done with care and genuine intent, carries more weight than splashy extravagance.

In business, company culture isn't defined by mission statements but shaped by daily behaviors. Fairness and care matter more than loud promises. A leader who listens with respect. A colleague who steps in when someone is overwhelmed. These are the "leaf and water" moments that build trust and emotional equity.

In relationships, the same applies. It's not the grand anniversary gift that builds connection—it's the moments of attention, the kept promises, and the quiet acts of care. These gestures say, "I see you. I value you. I'm here for you."

▶ *The scale of your effort matters less than the sincerity of your intention.*

This teaching also reframes how we think about contribution—what if we simply gave what we had, with sincerity? The ripple effect of honest contribution is often bigger than we realize.

Krishna's message here is liberating: You don't have to be perfect, powerful, or polished. You just have to be present—with sincerity.

The Power of Action as an Offering

Chapter 9, Verse 27: "Whatever is sacrificed, given, or done, and whatever austerity is practiced, must be done as an offering unto Me, O Arjun."

What makes action meaningful is not its scale but its sanctity. When done with the right intent, even the simplest act becomes elevated. Without that intent, even the grandest gestures lose their soul.

Yagna is a ritual of making offerings to the divine. Life, work, and business are each a *Yagna*—the metaphor is used here to represents a collective rhythmic effort for a purpose. When we approach our actions as offerings, effort transcends transaction. We transform the ordinary into the extraordinary.

➤ *The secret lies not in doing—but in doing it as an offering.*

What we do becomes *energy invested* in something greater than ourselves. We move from performance to presence. This is not ritualism—it's rhythm. Not hustle—but cadence. Not obligation— but conscious contribution.

➤ *Legacy is built on the care we embed, not just on the output we deliver.*

With this alchemy of **action-as-offering**, culture transforms. Teams no longer fulfill duties—they volunteer their best. Leaders stop demanding and start stewarding. Innovators create to solve rather than to sell. The exhaustion of "doing" gives way to the vitality of "building," because every action turns into an offering that carries the weight of intent.

Entrepreneurial Framework 9:

Hidden Market Insights & Visionary Thinking

Entrepreneurs should continue to innovate with sincerity and lead with purpose, serving the larger good of their customers, knowing that external factors are not entirely within their control.

Theme: Long-term vision should be seen as a commitment to creating value by innovating, while aligned to a larger purpose.

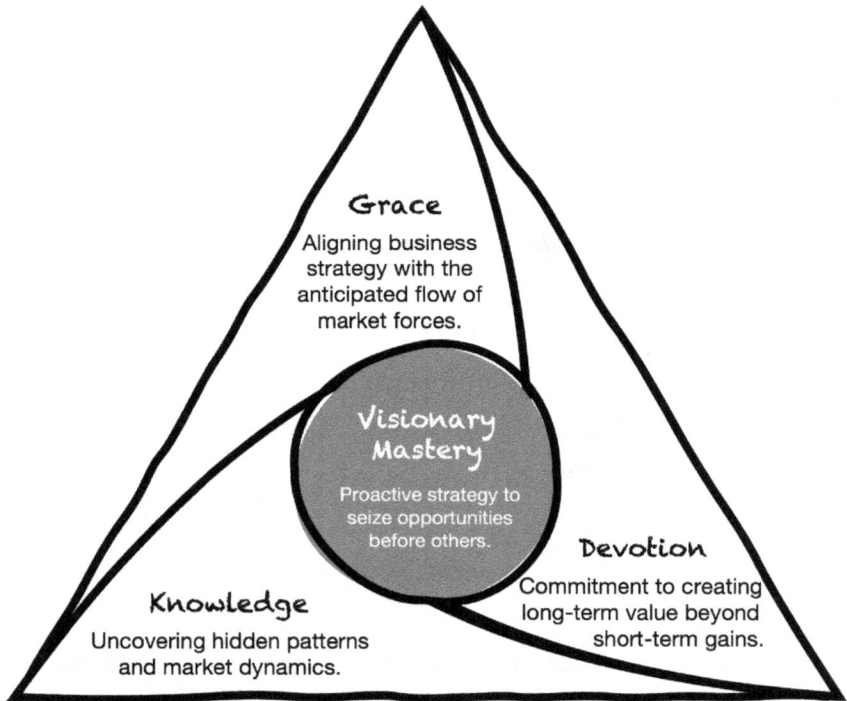

Grace
Aligning business strategy with the anticipated flow of market forces.

Visionary Mastery
Proactive strategy to seize opportunities before others.

Devotion
Commitment to creating long-term value beyond short-term gains.

Knowledge
Uncovering hidden patterns and market dynamics.

Business Insight:

Visionary entrepreneurs stand out not just for what they build but for what they *see*. They spot overlooked patterns, anticipate industry shifts, and stay ahead of the curve, because they are committed to creating long-term value.

➤ *The clearest insights often come from the quietest places—listening, observing, and staying aligned.*

What sets best founders apart is sincerity—a deep commitment to solving meaningful problems and creating a lasting impact. This isn't about virtue signaling. It's about contribution that endures.

This sincerity shapes company culture. Leaders who operate with care and clarity foster teams that innovate with purpose. They listen well, act with humility, and lead by example. The result? Organizations that are not only smart but also trusted.

Steve Jobs' ability to foresee the potential of smartphones with the iPhone wasn't just about innovation—it was driven by a deep belief in improving how people live and connect. It was rooted in product empathy and human understanding—a vision executed with care.

Action Step: When the market hums, leaders ask, "What's hiding here?" "How to ride the shift?" "Is there value for customers?" They think big but flow with purpose.

With **visionary thinking** in place, the next step is to build **brand power and influence**, which is explored in the next chapter.

Chapter 10
The Flow of Interconnectedness

The tenth chapter of the *Gita*, shifts the focus from inner mastery to the vastness of connection. Krishna reveals his presence as the vital force behind all existence and brilliance. He declares himself as the source of intellect, beauty, strength, order, and awe—manifesting in everything from the tiniest atom to the grandest galaxy. This is not philosophical; it is a revelation of how everything is connected.

Krishna invites Arjun to witness the lived expressions of consciousness and energy across all of nature and human endeavor and in everyday excellence. The brilliance of a great mind, the courage of a leader, the stability of a mountain, or the rhythm of a river—each of these is an expression of the same intelligent force moving through the universe. It is about recognizing the universal energy that drives the principles of existence. This understanding brings meaning to our lives to honor the deeper thread tying us all.

▶ *Greatness isn't outside us. It's within us, expressed when we're aligned with something bigger.*

This interconnectedness transforms modern leadership. Too often, we operate in silos—separating business from ethics, personal life from purpose, or success from service. But Krishna dissolves those lines, reminding us to align our actions with the greater flow of nature, of values, of purpose, to unlock creativity, resilience, and trust.

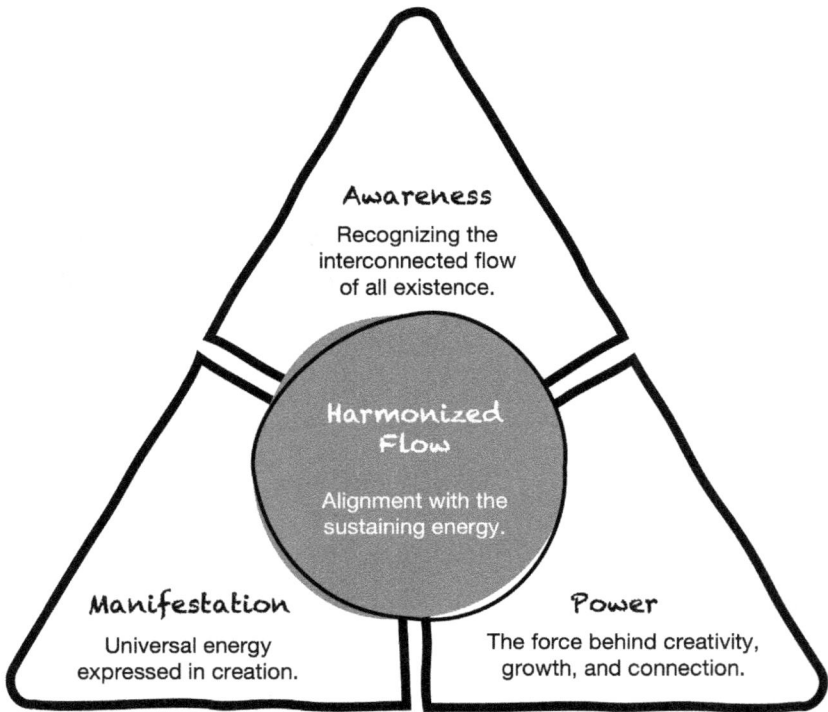

In business, this means designing solutions that serve both the customer and the planet. In leadership, it is making decisions that benefit both the profits and the people behind it. Interconnectedness doesn't reduce performance— it deepens it, grounding results in meaning.

In personal life, when we recognize the same life force in others, we become less transactional and more compassionate. Trust, collaboration, and shared success emerge naturally from this way of seeing.

For creators like artists, architects, or founders, this universal energy is an endless source of inspiration and creative spark. By aligning with this flow of common thread we touch people's hearts and blend devotion into craft.

Finding the Sacred in the Ordinary

Chapter 10, Verse 25: "Of sound vibrations I am Om, of sacrifices I am chanting the holy names, of immovable things I am the Himalayas."

Krishna reminds us that the sacred doesn't only live in scriptures or places of worship—it lives in the quiet design of the world around us. In sound, in rhythm, in nature, and in stillness. The sound of *Om* is the universal energy in its primal vibration. The Himalayas, symbolizing the majesty of nature, are expressions of this same universal energy that surrounds us. It is the presence of universal consciousness that moves through nature, systems, emotions, and relationships.

This verse invites us to tune into that energy. The way a clear voice inspires a room. The way a mountain calms the mind. The way a consistent rhythm of a ritual creates focus. These aren't mystical— they're deeply human. And they anchor us in something enduring.

➤ *Universal energy manifests through form and rhythm in everyday life.*

In leadership, this energy is expressed in subtle ways. A leader who stands firm like a mountain offers support and stability, setting the company's emotional climate. The cadence of regular rituals—team check-ins, values reviews, and reflective pauses—helps teams feel connected and centered.

Krishna's message is clear: the extraordinary doesn't lie far away—it pulses through the everyday. By honoring the sacred in sound, nature, and our actions, we elevate our consciousness and align with the greater flow of universal energy—leading to a life of harmony, presence, and purpose.

Inspiration Behind All Noble Actions

Chapter 10, Verse 39: "Wherever there is an enlivening, an exalting, and a righteous work, know that to be born of my Divine nature."

Krishna reminds us that wherever there is goodness, justice, or positive transformation, it is consciousness at play. It is a nudge to become agents of positive change, knowing even small efforts ripple outward into a cascading effect. True inspiration doesn't begin with us—it moves through us.

▶ *Purpose flows best when it's not about you—but moves through you.*

At work, choose integrity over convenience. In leadership, stand up for something even when unpopular. In design, build something useful, not just marketable. When our actions elevate others and solve real problems, we align with something greater than ourselves.

A helping hand, a quiet gesture of support, or a stand for fairness may seem modest, but these acts carry immense power. Our acts of kindness and compassion spread positive energy that lifts us and the world around us.

This isn't a call to perfection—it's an invitation to participate. Align with the flow; the work was never yours to own. In that surrender, something rare emerges: actions that fulfill us and resonate far beyond what we imagined.

Entrepreneurial Framework 10:

Brand Influence: Shaping Market Narratives

Entrepreneurs should understand the broader context in which a business operates and the intangibles that help to shape the business presence.

Theme: Purpose-driven influence of the brand power not just to compete but to inspire and shape industry narratives.

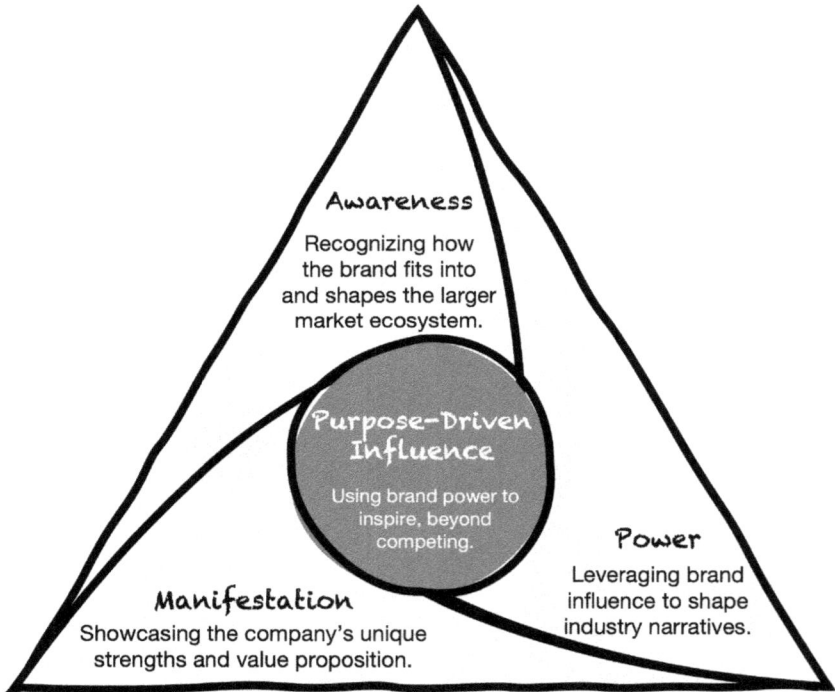

Awareness
Recognizing how the brand fits into and shapes the larger market ecosystem.

Purpose-Driven Influence
Using brand power to inspire, beyond competing.

Power
Leveraging brand influence to shape industry narratives.

Manifestation
Showcasing the company's unique strengths and value proposition.

Business Insight:

A strong brand is more than just awareness or positioning. It's a force that shapes conversations, expectations, and values—across customers, competitors, and communities. Market leaders don't just sell products—they define the playing field. And with that influence comes responsibility.

➤ *A brand's greatest asset isn't reach—it's resonance.*

Companies that wield brand influence don't just compete—they lead movements. They create long-term value, sustainable trust, and cultural relevance. They do this by anchoring in purpose to consistently deliver on what they stand for. Their messaging is not just clever—it's clear. Their values are not just statements—they are lived through choices, systems, and experiences.

As your brand grows, the stakes grow too. What you say—and don't say—shapes how the market sees you. The stronger the brand, the more people look to it not just for solutions but for direction. Your brand moves beyond competition to become indispensable. That's how visionary brands become legendary.

Nike's *"Just Do It"* didn't just market shoes. It inspired a culture of perseverance and athleticism. That kind of influence builds communities—not just customer bases.

Action Step: When brand influence grows, leaders ask, "What story shapes my market?" "How does it inspire others?" They steer with purpose, build something iconic.

With **brand power established**, the next step is to adopt **big-picture thinking**, which is explored in the next chapter.

Chapter 11
Seeing Beyond the Obvious

The eleventh chapter of the *Gita*, marks a dramatic turning point when Krishna grants Arjun divine sight to witness the Vision of the Universal Cosmic Form (*Vishvarup*). Arjun sees the scale, intensity, and interconnectedness of all things—and his own small place in the cosmic order. What unfolds is not a symbolic story but a transformational experience.

He no longer perceives Krishna as just a charioteer or mentor but as the all-encompassing force behind creation, action, and dissolution. This vision reveals that behind every act of creation, destruction, and transformation lies the same timeless force. It is a glimpse into the infinite nature of reality—a reality that includes us yet also vastly exceeds us.

This chapter isn't about mysticism—it's about perspective. Krishna reveals the larger context within which our choices, actions, and lives unfold. The moment is awe-inspiring, yet it is also deeply grounding. It reframes the battlefield, the decision, and the self.

➤ *Clarity often comes not from zooming in but from zooming way out.*

The message is clear: our lives are part of a greater flow. We're not isolated actors but participants in an interconnected whole. This encourages us to stay curious, to look deeper than what meets the eye, and to appreciate the bigger picture at play.

In the modern world, we often operate in narrow scopes: project deadlines, quarterly targets, and personal milestones. But Krishna's revelation pushes us to zoom out, look beyond that, and ask: *What are we really part of? What are our actions reinforcing or reshaping?*

At work, this teaching inspires us to think beyond limitations, embrace challenges, and recognize the great potential that lies within and around us. When we surrender to the vision of a bigger picture, we unlock our full potential to achieve amazing things.

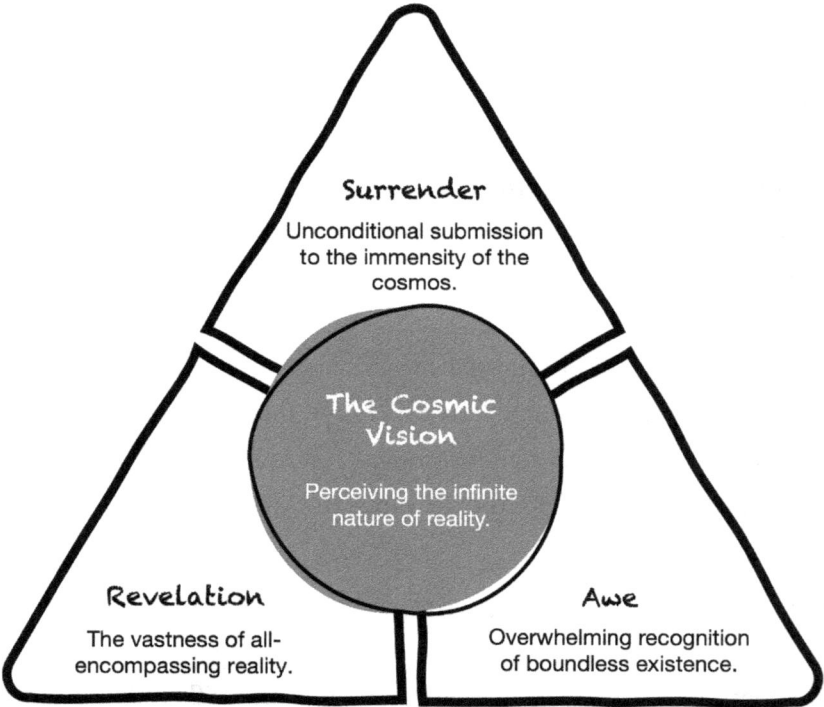

Surrender
Unconditional submission to the immensity of the cosmos.

The Cosmic Vision
Perceiving the infinite nature of reality.

Revelation
The vastness of all-encompassing reality.

Awe
Overwhelming recognition of boundless existence.

This broader view is strategic in business, leadership, and personal life. When we zoom out to see the whole, it aligns us with direction, not just movement. This perspective also deepens empathy. When we see others as part of the same whole—not obstacles or competitors, but fellow travelers—it reshapes how we lead, collaborate, and connect. It dissolves ego, giving way to trust and openness to forge bonds that truly matter.

The metaphor of cosmic vision is about understanding the larger design—we don't control everything, but we can choose how to consciously participate.

Achievement Through Grace-Inspired Effort

Chapter 11, Verse 48: "Neither by study of the Vedas, nor by austerity, nor by charity, nor by ritual can I be seen as you have seen Me."

Krishna makes a bold distinction. The full vision of reality cannot be accessed through knowledge, discipline, or good deeds alone—it is revealed through grace. When we are ready to see, open to receive, and willing to let go of control.

We're taught that hard work guarantees results, but there is more to it. Efforts matter, but that's only part of the equation. The greatest leaps in science, business, creativity, or life happen when we open ourselves to see beyond the apparent and remain ready to receive the unexpected. Not everything can be engineered. Some breakthroughs come when we stop pushing and start listening.

Love and connection cannot be forced through effort alone—they arise from openness. In leadership, too, those who are attuned to timing, intuition, and resonance are able to see the big picture.

▶ *Preparation creates the conditions. Grace delivers the moment.*

True visionary entrepreneurs are not those who work the hardest but those who remain open to inspiration, intuition, and wisdom that emerge beyond their plans. This could mean the timing of a market shift, the right investor alignment, or a product idea that feels intuitively right. These moments often emerge not through force but through flow. And leaders who learn to recognize that flow—who know when to lean in and when to allow—build with greater resilience.

Transformation happens when readiness meets receptivity. When we've done the work and are willing to release control, something greater can unfold. Prepare with effort, then open yourself to grace to bring the moments of transformation.

The Power of Loving Surrender

Chapter 11, Verse 54: "By devotion alone can I be thus known, truly known, and seen directly, Arjun. Take refuge in Me alone."

This verse is at the heart of the Gita's teaching: connection, not control, leads to real understanding. Krishna explains that through love, trust, and surrender—not intellect or force—we come into full awareness.

Our richest rewards come when we fully immerse ourselves in the journey rather than trying to control every turn. It is about belief in what we pursue. When we try to control every outcome, we exhaust ourselves. But when we commit with sincerity and release attachment, we begin to experience deeper impact, stronger relationships, and more meaningful results.

▶ *Devotion isn't weakness—it's focused engagement, free from ego.*

This principle shows up in teams that function with trust. In leaders who admit with sincerity what they don't know. In founders who care more about purpose than applause. These individuals operate from a deeper place—not just to win, but to contribute. In personal growth, it teaches us to let go of the urge to control, allowing ourselves to be shaped by experience, reflection, and humility.

Krishna's invitation is not to give up, but to give in to something larger than self-interest. The key to unlocking the universe's secrets lies in love, devotion, and surrender—that's how real power emerges.

Entrepreneurial Framework 11:

Big-Picture Thinking & Expanding Perspective

Entrepreneurship is about inside-out and outside-in thinking, the interconnectedness of the internal and external forces that shape the business.

Theme: Seeing interconnectedness in the broader market ecosystem to expand beyond immediate competition.

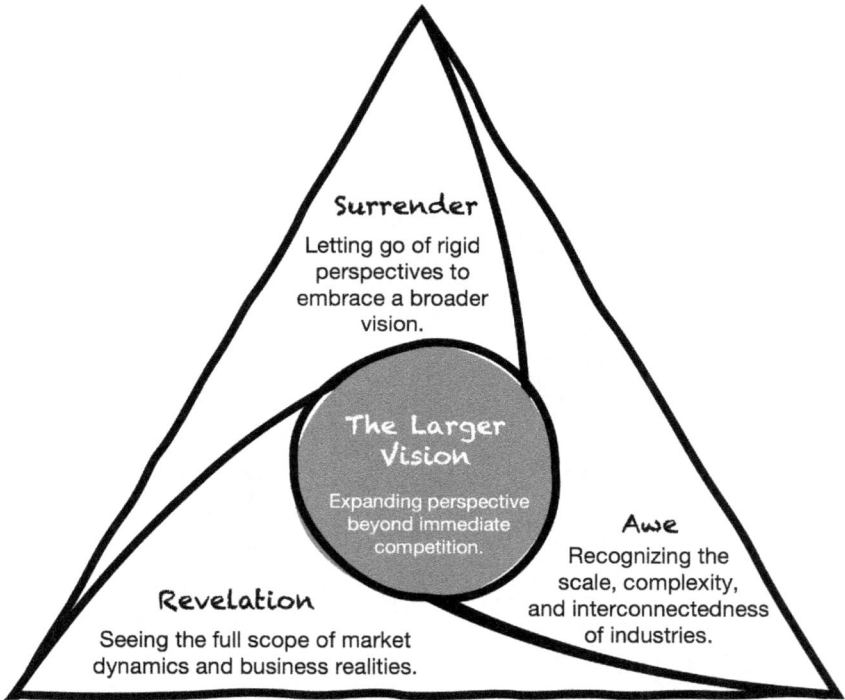

Surrender
Letting go of rigid perspectives to embrace a broader vision.

The Larger Vision
Expanding perspective beyond immediate competition.

Awe
Recognizing the scale, complexity, and interconnectedness of industries.

Revelation
Seeing the full scope of market dynamics and business realities.

Business Insight:

Early-stage startups operate with a sharp focus on product-market fit, customer acquisition, and operations. But as the companies grow, so must the perspective of the founders. When they begin to look beyond the confines of their current PMF, they often discover that their true market potential is a much larger opportunity beyond their initial assumptions.

➤ *When you see only the customer, you miss the market. When you see the ecosystem, you build for impact.*

The real advantage lies in the ability to zoom out and see the whole landscape: new markets, ecosystem shifts, global trends, regulatory waves, and evolving customer values. Founders who embrace this big-picture perspective are better positioned to anticipate disruptions and seize new opportunities to drive long-term growth.

Visionary leaders step back regularly to ask, *How is our market evolving beyond our current customer base? Are we building for today's demand—or tomorrow's expectations?*

It takes humility, curiosity, and the discipline to pause and zoom out—even when the current model seems to be working.

Amazon's evolution from a bookstore to a global commerce and cloud infrastructure powerhouse is a masterclass in big-picture thinking. It wasn't just about breadth—it was about anticipating where value would emerge and positioning the business ahead of it.

Action Step: When planning for scale, ask, "What holds our market together?" "What defines the next wave?" "Who will be our future customer?" Zoom out, think possibilities, build for what's next.

With a **broader perspective** in place, the next step is to **lead with purpose and commitment**, which is explored in the next chapter.

Chapter 12
The Joy and Purpose Beyond Self

The twelfth chapter of the *Gita*, Krishna goes deeper into the Path of Devotion *(Bhakti)* and focuses on the attitude of the devotee—how one should cultivate love, humility, and detachment in daily life.

Krishna's portrait of an ideal devotee is simple: calm in chaos, steady in discomfort, free from envy, gentle in strength, committed yet detached. These qualities may sound simple, but they require strength because they are not about performance. They're about embodiment, about how they're lived. This practice isn't loud or reactive. It's quietly consistent and grounded.

➤ *Devotion is doing your work with care—even when no one is watching.*

It is about cultivating a mindset of unconditional devotion that comes from love and surrender. It is immersion beyond transaction that comes from deep commitment. It is love in the form of unwavering worship. It can be expressed not only through prayers but also by living these values in the rhythm of daily life.

Often, we are drawn into this practice subconsciously, simply because we found something worth serving. When we are aligned with what matters, the work pulls us. Not with pressure but with quiet joy. It's not urgency but eagerness—gentle anticipation to return to something meaningful, where every task becomes an offering rather than a chore.

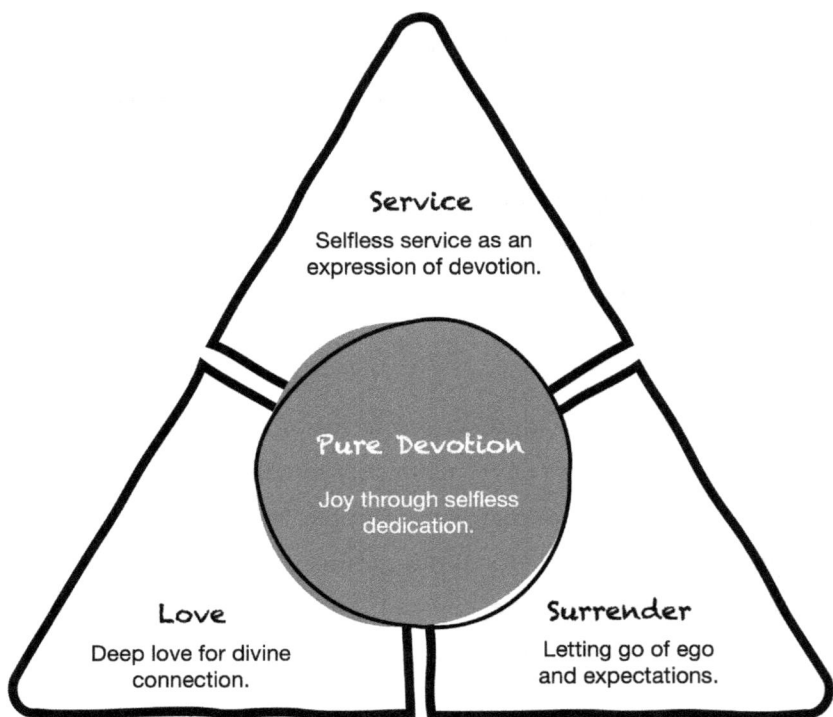

Service
Selfless service as an expression of devotion.

Pure Devotion
Joy through selfless dedication.

Love
Deep love for divine connection.

Surrender
Letting go of ego and expectations.

It translates into a deep commitment to a cause, passion, or values. Devoted entrepreneurs don't just build companies—they build missions that matter. A sincere leader who truly cares earns trust that no title can command. A committed professional who takes pride in uplifting others creates culture. A creator who pours love into their craft creates work that touches people—because it is built with intention, not just ambition.

➤ *Commitment at work is measured in care, not ceremony.*

Through the love for work, this practice turns work into worship. And when outcomes wobble and uncertainty looms, it reminds us to stay anchored—not in control, but in commitment. When the going gets tough, committed entrepreneurs don't give up, they hold firm to serve their vision and live their values.

This chapter invites us to infuse purpose into how we live and work. This path doesn't make life easier, but it shifts our focus from the struggle to control to the joy of alignment with our values, our service, our mission. We walk with quiet certainty, knowing we are a part of something far greater than ourselves.

Devotion: The Journey Beyond the Obvious

Chapter 12, Verses 6-7: "Those who set their hearts on Me as their supreme goal, worshiping Me with steadfast devotion—to them I deliver self-realization from the ocean of birth and death."

Krishna assures that steady devotion brings freedom. It's not about intensity—it's about consistency. Not occasional effort, but steady presence. When we direct our heart and actions toward something that brings us meaning, we begin to dissolve the distractions, doubts, and attachments that keep us stuck.

This is about staying true to your **north star**—a goal or purpose that provides direction even when the path is unclear. The people who achieve the deepest sense of fulfillment are those who stay committed. They find their edge, fall in love with the process, and build grit through grace—even when it's hard.

➤ *Progress doesn't come from perfection. It comes from staying in the game with love.*

In leadership, we see this in founders who carry their vision through storms, not just sunshine. In teams that stay united through turmoil. In individuals who grow by deepening their craft. Growth comes from devotion—not drama.

Krishna's teaching is clear: devotion is love with discipline, not blind faith. And that kind of devoted commitment carries us forward—through fear, through fatigue, and into freedom. It outlasts uncertainty.

The Power of Empathy and Compassion

Chapter 12, Verse 16: "He who harbors no ill will toward any being, who is friendly and compassionate, free from egoism—he is dear to Me."

This verse sharpens the spotlight on character over competence. Krishna reveals that the true devotee is defined not by knowledge or achievements, but by how they live. Empathy, compassion, and humility aren't soft traits, they are indicators of mature and evolved leadership.

In a world of scale, speed, and strategy, it's easy to lose the human dimension. Yet what people remember, whether in teams, families, or communities, is how they were treated. Respect, kindness, and fairness build trust that no amount of execution or strategy can replicate.

▶ *Good leaders don't just move things forward—they lift people up along the way.*

Professionals who lead with compassion resolve conflict faster, retain talent longer, and create environments where innovation thrives. Relationships deepen when built on sincerity rather than transaction. And cultures thrive when ego takes a back seat to mutual respect.

Krishna's message? When we drop ego, we make room for connection. When we lead with care, we create impact. When we live this way consistently, we don't just succeed—we become the kind of people others trust, follow, and remember.

Entrepreneurial Framework 12:

Purpose-Driven Leadership: Where Devotion Meets Impact

Entrepreneurs should exercise self-control to stay focused, lead with unwavering dedication, and let the purpose-driven commitment turn vision into reality.

Theme: Commitment to mission-driven growth and inspiring teams through shared purpose.

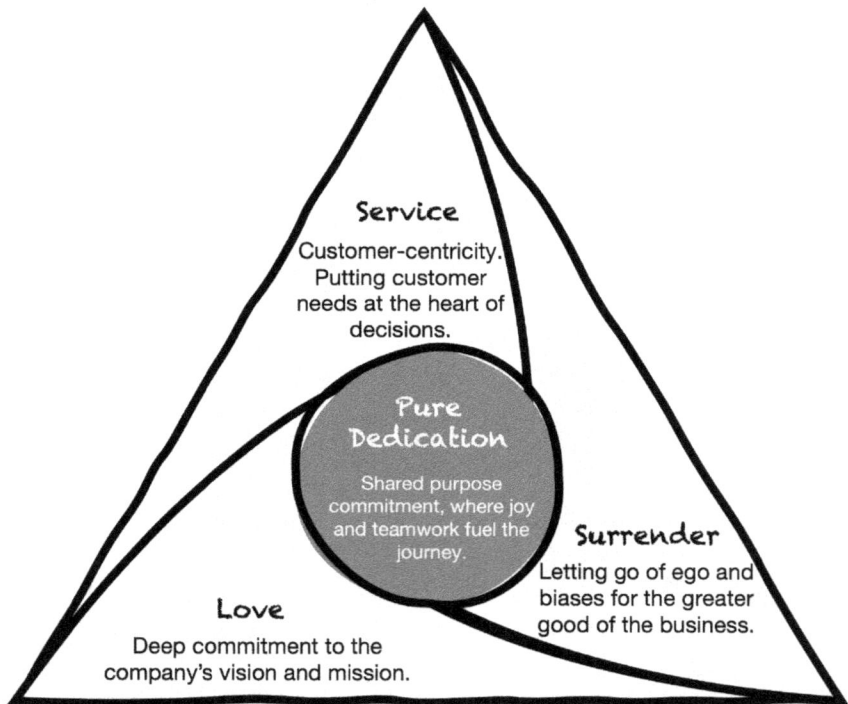

Service
Customer-centricity. Putting customer needs at the heart of decisions.

Pure Dedication
Shared purpose commitment, where joy and teamwork fuel the journey.

Surrender
Letting go of ego and biases for the greater good of the business.

Love
Deep commitment to the company's vision and mission.

Business Insight:

The most successful founders aren't only driven by product, performance, or profit—they're driven by a deep love for their mission. They lead from conviction. They are devoted to what they believe in, and that belief shapes how they navigate complexity, hire teams, and serve customers.

➤ *Devotion to purpose deepens resolve, simplifies decisions.*

These leaders don't operate from ego. They stay curious, listen closely, and remain open to being wrong—because their loyalty is to the mission, not personal pride. They balance customer focus with long-term integrity. And they build cultures where mission, not micromanagement, drives performance.

This kind of leadership inspires people, builds resilience through hard seasons and garners support during inflection points. Culture becomes a competitive advantage, not through slogans, but how things are done every day.

Yvon Chouinard, founder of Patagonia, led with purpose from day one. His commitment to environmental sustainability is concrete proof of devotion-as-strategy. It shaped everything—from product decisions and messaging to hiring and operations. Such devotion creates alignment—and alignment creates momentum.

Action Step: When purpose calls, leaders ask, "What lifts my team?" "What drives my mission?" "What serves my customers?" They stay true, inspire fully, and build lasting joy.

With **purpose-driven leadership** in place, the next step is to **cultivate self-awareness**, which is explored in the next chapter.

Chapter 13
Understanding the Eternal and the Transient

The thirteenth chapter of the *Gita*, offers a powerful framework for self-awareness to navigating change with clarity. Krishna distinguishes between the **Field** *(Kshetra)*—our body, mind, emotions, and environment—and the **Knower of the Field** *(Kshetrajna)*—the eternal consciousness that witnesses it without being entangled.

This duality helps us differentiate between what is transient and what is eternal: *what changes and what never will.* In a world of constant motion, this insight becomes our anchor. Our roles, routines, and external identities are always evolving, but beneath them lies a steady awareness. When we recognize this, we lead with presence to avoid being consumed by every shift.

➤ *Anchoring in what lasts helps you move wisely through what changes.*

This separation between the transient and the eternal is the foundation of resilience. When we identify only with the **field**, our achievements, possessions, or reputation, we become reactive and restless. But when we act from the vantage point of the **knower**, we meet gain and loss with equal composure.

In personal life, this means cherishing relationships, successes, and experiences without clinging, knowing they are impermanent. In career, it means striving for growth while recognizing that titles and outcomes don't define us. This is equanimity *(Samatva)* in action—the wisdom to welcome success and failure as passing seasons.

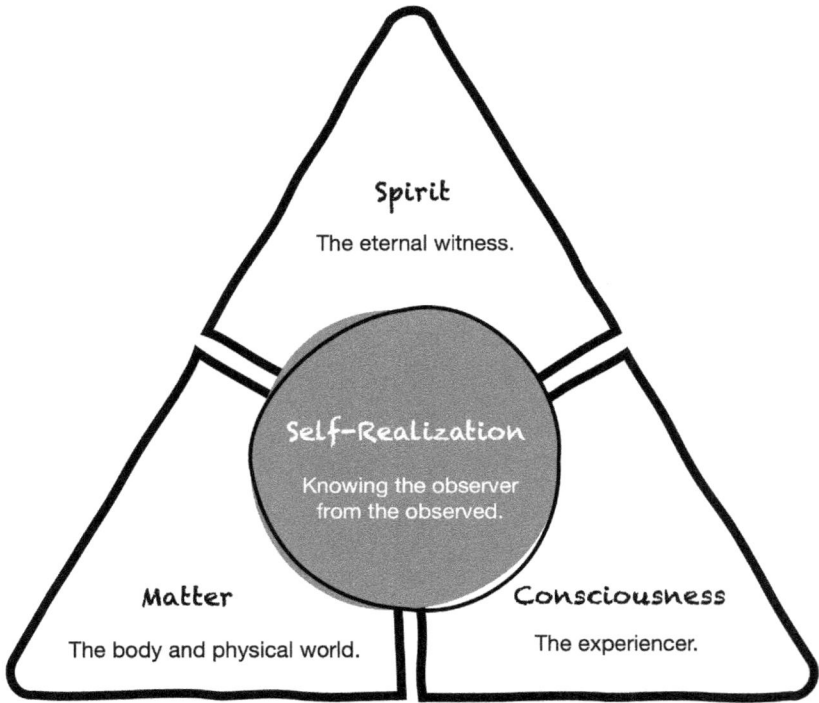

Spirit
The eternal witness.

Self-Realization
Knowing the observer
from the observed.

Matter
The body and physical world.

Consciousness
The experiencer.

In business, the **Field** is operations, markets, and customer behavior, which is chaos in motion. The **Knower** is the mission, values, and purpose—the inner compass that stays constant and survives every storm. Leaders who grasp this don't confuse turbulence with direction. They don't panic at every market turn because they know what must evolve and what must endure.

At the heart of this teaching lies **discernment** *(Vivek)*. Knowing what to hold and what to release. What to adapt and what to protect. This is the wisdom that frees us: to act fully in the world yet never lose ourselves to it.

Virtues for a Purposeful Life

Chapter 13, Verse 8: "Humility, authenticity, nonviolence, forgiveness, integrity, service, devotion—the qualities that lead to oneness with Brahman."

Krishna shares a list of virtues—not as moral prescriptions, but as traits that fuse clarity with impact. These aren't abstract ideals, they're life and leadership assets.

- **Humility** opens us to feedback and growth.
- **Authenticity** aligns word and action to build trust.
- **Nonviolence** de-escalates conflict with empathy and calm.
- **Forgiveness** clears emotional residue to heal faster.
- **Integrity** builds reputation over the long haul.
- **Service** turns ambition into contribution.
- **Devotion** anchors work in purpose.

In business, these virtues shape culture—from how decisions are made to how people are treated. Leaders who embody them build legacies. Teams rooted in service out-innovate competitors better because they build with care. People who lead with authenticity and integrity create ecosystems where trust compounds.

➤ *Success without character is fragile. Character without action is wasted.*

In relationships, these values foster depth, safety, and understanding. In personal growth, they keep us grounded when ego tempts us to drift. In work, they shape culture, deepen loyalty, and create space where people don't just perform—they belong.

This verse isn't about perfection—it's about orientation: building from ego vs. from alignment. These virtues are the quiet engines of enduring success.

Embracing Oneness Through Equality and Empathy

Chapter 13, Verse 28: "He who sees the omnipresent Supreme Lord existing equally within all perishable beings truly sees."

Krishna expands the lens of awareness by introducing oneness (*Advaita*) or non-duality. He unveils the deeper truth: the Field and Knower are the two layers of the same reality. While the forms we see differ, the essence within is the same and eternal. Recognizing that shared essence transforms how we lead, relate, and live.

When we argue with a colleague, compete with a rival, or judge ourselves, we're seeing only the Field—the visible surface. But beneath roles, opinions, and mistakes lies the same essence. This perspective of oneness builds empathy. It shifts conflicts into connections and pride into understanding. The leader and the intern, the customer and the supplier, the employee and the founder—all carry the same spark. This awareness builds resilience, it shifts conflicts into connections and pride into understanding.

▶ *When we see people for who they are—not just what they do—we lead with care, not control.*

In business, this means designing systems that respect duality (roles, hierarchies, KPIs) while seeing beyond it to nurture a culture of oneness through mentorship and equity. The balance of unity in the duality. This shows up in humanized cultures, equitable systems, and leaders who listen deeply.

In relationships, it creates space for patience, generosity, and forgiveness. And in personal growth, it means not judging ourselves too harshly when we stumble—reminding us that mistakes don't diminish our worth.

The world around may change, but the essence remains the same. When we connect with that truth, in others and in ourselves, we become less reactive, more patient, and far more effective in both life and leadership. That's when we truly begin to lead.

Entrepreneurial Framework 13:

Centered Leadership: Awareness, Discernment & Balance

Entrepreneurs must lead with both precision and perspective—understanding the difference between what needs to adapt and what must remain constant.

Theme: Leading with clarity through self-awareness—discerning markets from the mission.

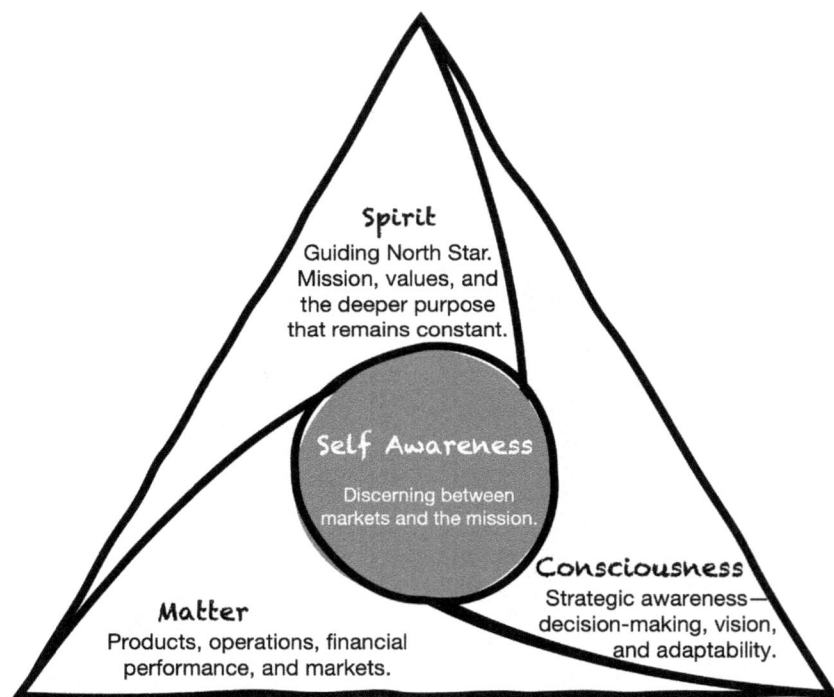

Spirit
Guiding North Star. Mission, values, and the deeper purpose that remains constant.

Self Awareness
Discerning between markets and the mission.

Consciousness
Strategic awareness— decision-making, vision, and adaptability.

Matter
Products, operations, financial performance, and markets.

Business Insight:

In fast-paced environments, it's easy to get swept up by shifting markets, feedback loops, and operational fires. But centered leaders pause. They separate signal from noise. They lead from a place of discernment—mastering duality in action. They know that business operations *(matter)* are always in motion, but strategic clarity *(consciousness)* and a deeper mission *(spirit)* must remain anchored.

▶ *Great strategy starts with inner stability.*

The ability to distinguish what is enduring (vision, culture, integrity) from what is circumstantial (tools, platforms, pricing models) is a strategic superpower. Centered leaders don't react to every wave. They recognize which ones to ride and which ones to let pass. This awareness enables leaders to pivot without compromising purpose.

Oprah Winfrey's ability to pivot from talk show host to media mogul while staying true to her mission of empowerment shows self-awareness in leadership.

Action Step: When complexity rises, ask, "What will change?" "What remains true?" Center first—then lead.

With self-**awareness** established, the next step is to master the **balance of forces shaping business evolution**, which is explored in the next chapter.

Chapter 14
Transcending the Forces That Shape Us

The fourteenth chapter of the *Gita,* brings back the focus on the three invisible currents running through every decision, relationship, and system. Lifting some, dragging others, and keeping a few suspended. These fundamental forces of nature are Sattva, bringing ethics, purity, and balance; Rajas, driving ambition, passion, and activity; and Tamas, creating inertia, ignorance, and stagnation. These primal energies *(Gunas)* shape everything—from thoughts to civilizations. They are not fixed; they shift in people, businesses, and even economies, shaping how we decide, connect, and grow.

▶ *We're not static beings—we're shaped by shifting forces that color how we act and lead.*

Sattva brings clarity, purpose, and fairness. Yet too much of it can pull us away from execution, making well-meaning visionaries drift from practical responsibilities.

Rajas is the fire of ambition, creativity, and action—the drive to build, win, and scale. But left unchecked, it becomes restlessness, ego, and burnout.

Tamas, often misunderstood, also brings rest, recovery, and reflection. But when dominant, it becomes inertia, resistance, and delay.

We are not to eliminate these forces—but to observe them, balance them, and rise above their pull. Understanding them sharpens self-awareness.

A *Rajasic* mindset fuels bold moves but may trigger stress and discontent when tied to external wins. A *Tamasic* approach calls for undue caution and comfort-zone thinking, blocking growth. A *Sattvic* mindset enables integrity and purpose—but may avoid rewards and recognition that are essential to visibility and influence. The key is not to choose one but to strike the right balance: the energy of *Rajas*, clarity of *Sattva*, and stability from the inertia of *Tamas*.

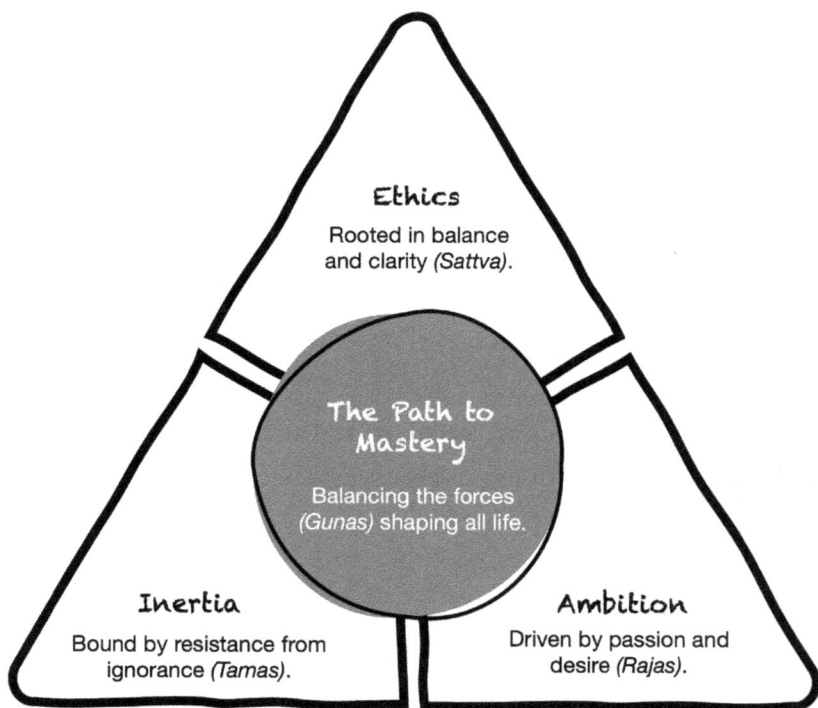

Ethics
Rooted in balance
and clarity *(Sattva)*.

The Path to Mastery
Balancing the forces
(Gunas) shaping all life.

Inertia
Bound by resistance from
ignorance *(Tamas)*.

Ambition
Driven by passion and
desire *(Rajas)*.

➤ *The wise don't reject the Gunas; they conduct them.*

The *Gunas* don't just shape individuals—they define entire organizations.

A *Sattvic* one prioritizes ethics and vision, but without *Rajas*, it's all compass, no engine.

A *Rajasic* one thrives on speed and dominance, but without *Sattva*, it's a rocket without a guidance system.

A *Tamasic* one clings to comfort, but without *Rajas* and *Sattva*, it's a ship stuck in harbor, stable yet stagnant.

The sweet spot is the right balance: *Sattva* for direction, *Rajas* for momentum, and *Tamas* for consolidation. Awareness is the first step to rebalance: *What's your workplace running on—and what's running it?*

▶ *The future belongs to those who know when to push, pause, or pivot.*

Krishna's call isn't to escape the *Gunas* but to learn to dance with them, rising above their pull, aware enough to lead, not follow. When we observe their play without being played by them, we act from freedom, not force. And that's where true power begins—with intention, not compulsion.

Be the Player, Not the Pawn

Chapter 14, Verse 9: "The three modes—goodness, passion, ignorance—all come from Me. I am not within them, they are within Me."

The three primal energies are like waves arising from the ocean— they shape our emotions, actions, and thoughts, but we need not remain trapped in their hold. Moralizing them as good or bad misses Krishna's insight. *Tamas* isn't evil; it's the pause between breaths. *Sattva* isn't *virtue*; it's the light that can blind as much as guide. They are not prescriptions but energies to be understood, orchestrated, and ultimately transcended.

▶ *Maturity is knowing when and how to balance reflection, momentum, and restraint.*

Like seasons, businesses and economies too move through the cycles of these forces of nature. Wise leaders recognize these shifts and adapt. A *Rajasic* sprint—rapid expansion, intense ambition—needs *Sattvic* ethics to avoid recklessness. A *Tamasic* slump—rigidity, stagnation—demands *Rajas'* push to reignite and a *Sattvic* vision to reinvent. Even *Sattvic* vision dies without *Rajas* to execute and *Tamas* to stabilize.

▶ *The Gunas may move through us—but we choose whether they drive us.*

In careers, *Rajas* may thrive in sales and startups, *Sattva* in research or teaching, and *Tamas* in operations or systems. But none of them stay dominant forever. We make space for them, but we are not their prisoner—they do not define us. Instead of staying stuck in one mode, learn to flex based on what the moment calls for. This understanding builds emotional strength.

Dedication Transcends Forces

Chapter 14, Verse 26: "One who serves with unwavering dedication rises above these forces and is ready for higher awareness."

126

Krishna reveals that the path to transcendence is not through isolation, suppression, or denial, but through unwavering dedication. And that means steady, focused service. It's about consistency: showing up with sincerity, anchored in purpose, not swayed by mood or mode.

▶ *Stability comes not from perfection but from steady contribution.*

In today's language, we may call this "flow" or "being in the zone," but it is deeper than that. When we immerse ourselves in action with devotion—not for outcomes or applause, but from sincerity—we rise above the sway of the three primal energies, the *Gunas*.

Whether building a company, supporting a team, raising a child, or learning a craft—staying with it, without expectation, is the way upward. Business leaders tied to a real purpose, whether it's sustainability, innovation, or customer well-being, rise above market noise and volatility. They build long-term influence. Entrepreneurs dedicated to creating meaningful impact build organizations that outlast fads, downturns, and hype.

▶ *We create significance when we do our work with undistracted sincerity.*

In life, this means not succumbing to the emotional whiplash of highs and lows. Instead, commit to work that builds with care, relationships that grow with time, and a life that leaves a legacy. Not dropping ambition but rising above it with awareness.

By showing up undistracted and with dedication, we transcend fleeting influences to live with fulfillment and purpose.

Entrepreneurial Framework 14:

Business Balance: Vision, Execution & Stability

Successful entrepreneurs balance vision, execution, and stability—adapting to change with clarity, not compulsion, while staying rooted in their core mission.

Theme: Self-mastery by balancing vision with pivot, push, and pause to avoid isolation, burnout, or stagnation.

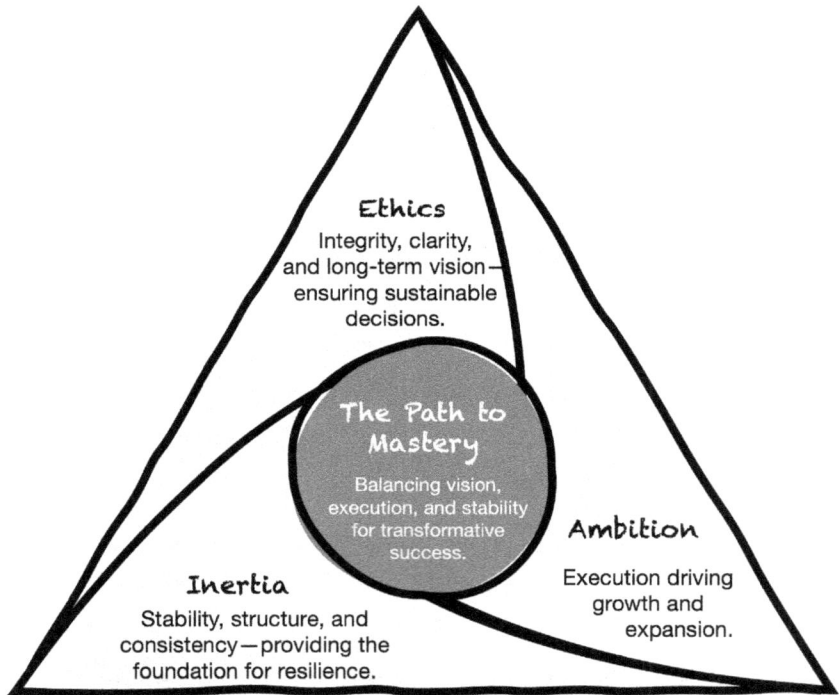

Ethics
Integrity, clarity, and long-term vision—ensuring sustainable decisions.

The Path to Mastery
Balancing vision, execution, and stability for transformative success.

Ambition
Execution driving growth and expansion.

Inertia
Stability, structure, and consistency—providing the foundation for resilience.

Business Insight:

High-performing founders often operate on hustle. But sustained leadership isn't about doing more—it's about understanding what's driving your decisions. When you pause to assess your internal state, you stop being reactive and start becoming responsive. You shift from operating on instinct to leading with intention.

➤ *What drives you shapes what you build.*

Every business moves through cycles of energy. *Rajas* is dominant in the startup phase—speed, risk-taking, and bold pivots. *Tamas* sets in during prolonged periods of steady operations—comfort, inertia, and bureaucratic drag. *Sattva* can emerge in companies with strong vision and values.

Founders who learn to manage these patterns across teams, cultures, and product life cycles gain a deeper edge. They know when to pause, when to push, and when to pivot.

Apple is an example of a company that harmonized all three modes. *Sattva* inspired elegant design and user-centric thinking. *Rajas* drove rapid innovation and global expansion. *Tamas* anchored operational scale and reliability. The balance wasn't by default—but by design.

Action Step: When forces shift, leaders ask, "What grounds my vision?" "What fuels my drive?" "What holds my ground?" They balance wisely, act aware, and build with intent.

With the **mastery of balancing the forces**, the next step is to **cut through illusions** for lasting impact, which is explored in the next chapter.

Chapter 15
Cutting Through Illusion to Gain Mastery

The fifteenth chapter of the *Gita*, explores the inverted nature of human perception, using the metaphor of an upside-down *Ashvattha* tree (a type of fig tree) with roots above and branches below.

Let's call this the "Illusory Tree"—with branches extending downward into the material world, fed by human desires, binding us to a cycle of longing and struggle (*Samsara*). Its leaves represent the rituals and scriptures that cannot alone give us freedom from the cycle. The true nourishment for life lies in the roots above.

▶ *The world looks upright—but we're growing downward if we forget where we're rooted.*

This tree is seductive—its beauty distracts us from its illusion. We climb its branches—chasing success, relationships, pleasure, and power—only to discover that the fruit never fully satisfies.

Krishna's solution? Cut the tree with an axe of detachment—to discern the truth and release the illusion. To act without entanglement, to the root where real nourishment lies.

➤ *Cutting the tree doesn't mean renouncing life—it means refusing to stay lost in it.*

In business and leadership, we often climb higher without checking what we're rooted in. Titles, scale, visibility, and valuation are the branches we mistake for meaning. Without strong roots of vision, values, and service, we drift or break.

Krishna introduces *Purushottam*—the still, eternal presence within us that witnesses all but is not seduced or shaken by it. Contrast this with the lower Self, where we live most of our lives—chasing, defending, reacting. The invitation is to awaken to the higher Self— calm, spacious, and aligned.

Krishna, the universal consciousness and energy, shines in the sun and moon, sustains all life, and resides in each one of us. This instills humility: all success emerges from interconnected universal order— never fully self-made. This encourages ethical and sustainable practices by reinforcing that all resources are shared and we should use them wisely.

➤ *We rise by remembering who we are within it.*

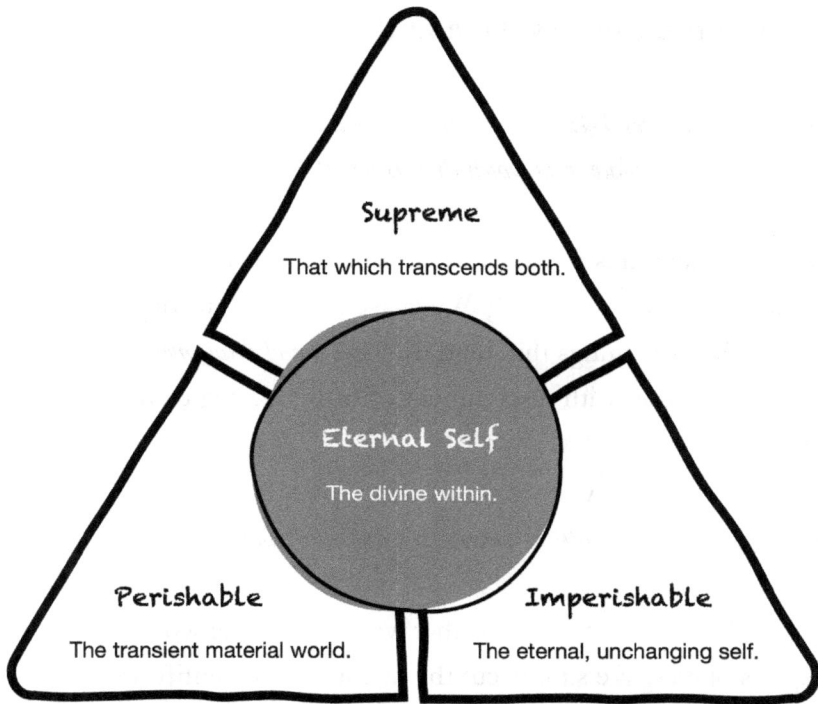

Supreme
That which transcends both.

Eternal Self
The divine within.

Perishable
The transient material world.

Imperishable
The eternal, unchanging self.

This chapter is a call to mature vision. We can live in the world, lead with ambition, and still be anchored in what doesn't change. Cutting the tree is a metaphor for this maturity. Once seen through the illusion, we can still climb—but now, from a grounded place.

This chapter further extends this teaching to present a powerful contrast: the perishable (*Kshara*) and the imperishable (*Akshara*). The body, roles, and material world are perishable—subject to decay and disruption. But the Self is imperishable, eternal—unmoved by status, undiminished by loss. This is not an escape from ambition but an elevation of it. When we root our identity in the perishable, we become anxious and reactive. When we act from the imperishable, we lead with calm and clarity. The swing of the axe is daily—cutting the branches and climbing with the roots.

Cutting the Illusory Tree at the Root

Chapter 15, Verses 3-4: "Only when the tree is cut with the axe of detachment does one reach the place from which there is no return."

The call to action is to cut the tree of illusion that entangles us in distraction, ego, and striving. We chase its fruits but forget its roots—the very things that bind us. The *axe of detachment* cuts through delusion with discernment of truth, freeing us from sensory traps.

▶ *Detachment isn't walking away—it's knowing what not to cling to.*

The *Gita* has never advocated that we abandon the world or its responsibilities. We simply cut the unconscious identification with the temporary. The *place of no return* is not a physical destination but a state of consciousness where actions flow from inner alignment, not conditioned impulse. We still live, act, and build, but with awareness, and we no longer serve the tree of illusion.

▶ *The deeper the root, the stronger the tree—even when the weather turns.*

Companies that solve for root causes, not just surface symptoms, build offerings that matter. In doing so, they become resilient— because they draw from something deeper than market cycles or quarterly metrics.

▶ *You don't transcend illusion by rearranging it. You do it by tracing back to the source.*

Krishna's challenge: Stop climbing. Cut clean. Then begin. That's how we turn inward—where purpose outshines performance, and being replaces becoming.

The Inner Source of Wisdom and Light

Chapter 15, Verse 15: "I am seated in the hearts of all living beings. Memory, knowledge, as well as their loss come from Me."

Krishna reveals that the light we seek outside is already within us. It isn't a distant force but an inner guide. True understanding doesn't come from external inputs alone but from moments of quiet illumination within—through clarity, intuition, and alignment with something deeper within.

➤ *The light we seek outside is already active within.*

This teaching speaks directly to our capacity for intuitive knowledge—beyond intellect or logic. Even in the age of infinite data, our most profound insights often arrive when we silence the noise and listen inward. This isn't mysticism—it is subconscious integration at work beneath the surface. The answers we seek are often already within us, waiting to be revealed. Many of history's greatest innovators and leaders—from Einstein to Gandhi—credited their breakthroughs not just to intellect but to inner conviction.

➤ *Innovation often begins as a whisper—not a formula.*

While data remains vital, great leaders know when to pause the spreadsheets and dashboards to listen inward. That's where clarity lives. They let go of outdated assumptions—and in that space, new insights emerge from the same inner source. Practices like reflection, meditation, or even journaling connect us to the inner guidance system. The more we cultivate inner awareness, the more confidently we can pivot, persist, or pursue bold moves—often long before external signals catch up.

▶ *Data provides the map, but intuition points to true north.*

Krishna's verse invites intellectual humility. When we see ourselves as a channel through which insights and achievements flow, it softens the ego. We connect inward and make more meaningful contributions.

Entrepreneurial Framework 15:

Rooted Strategy: First Principles Over Flash

Smart entrepreneurs lead with intuition, validate with data, and anchor in first principles before metrics guide their course.

Theme: Cut illusions and anchor in core with first principles, not just speed of execution.

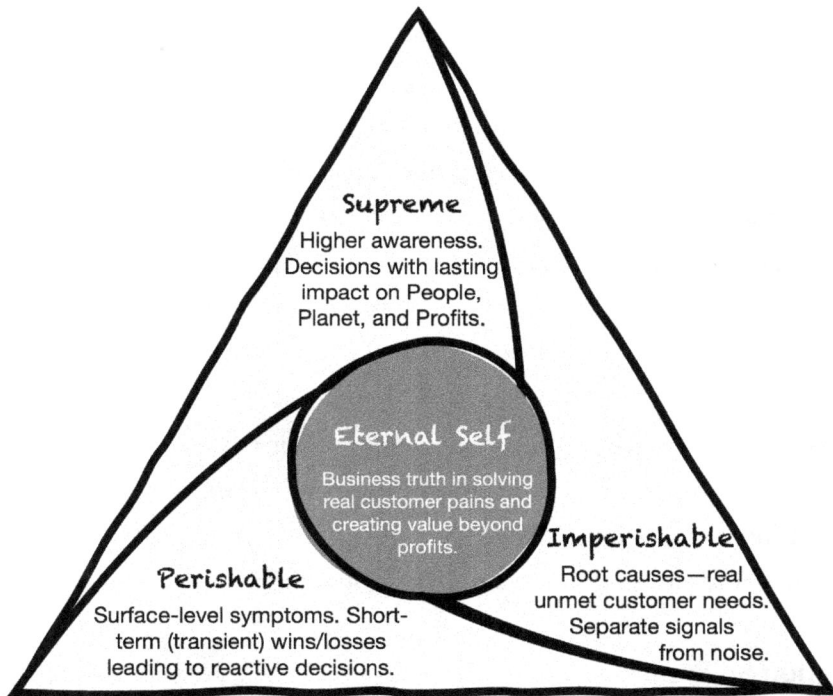

Supreme
Higher awareness. Decisions with lasting impact on People, Planet, and Profits.

Eternal Self
Business truth in solving real customer pains and creating value beyond profits.

Imperishable
Root causes—real unmet customer needs. Separate signals from noise.

Perishable
Surface-level symptoms. Short-term (transient) wins/losses leading to reactive decisions.

Business Insight:

Startups are often seduced by the visible—growth, reach, and valuation. Founders who fixate on perishable metrics—virality, vanity KPIs, quarterly spikes—may rise fast, but their success is brittle. The real advantage lies in anchoring to the imperishable: unmet needs, first principles, and timeless customer truths.

During market volatility, purpose-driven leaders return to first principles. They think like gardeners—they prune what no longer serves. They don't chase the spotlight—they cultivate strength from within. That clarity empowers them to manage their pace, pivot when necessary, and cut illusions before illusions cut them.

▶ *Illusion looks like traction when you're not watching the root.*

Let your product roadmap, pricing model, and growth strategy evolve, but stay rooted in your purpose, principles, and values. If they weaken, everything above will eventually collapse. This is the cornerstone of entrepreneurial decision-making. Don't copy rivals, innovate from within, scale what resonates, and let go of what no longer serves.

Tesla's focus on solving the global energy crisis through sustainable transportation and energy is a masterclass in first principles thinking. By stripping away long-held assumptions, they cut through illusion to build a future rooted in clarity, not convention.

Action Step: In your next strategic review, ask, "Are we building depth or chasing drama?" "What's valuable and what's just visible?" "First principles or rival mimicry?" Grow true, grow tall, grow lasting.

With **illusions dispelled**, the next step is to **rise above destructive competition** through **ethical leadership**, which is explored in the next chapter.

Chapter 16
The Fork: Integrity vs. Exploitation

The sixteenth chapter of the *Gita* offers a practical map of character and conduct. Krishna outlines two paths: the *Divine* or Virtuous that elevates and integrates, and the *Demonic* or Vicious that distorts and divides.

The virtuous path blooms with courage, self-restraint, empathy, truthfulness, and patience. These create expansion and harmony, ground us in purpose, and support long-term well-being. The vicious path grows from arrogance, deceit, anger, harshness, and manipulation. These may deliver short-term results but eventually create distortion, instability, and harm.

An old Cherokee once told his grandson,

"My son, there is a battle between two wolves inside us all.

One is Evil.

It is anger, jealousy, greed, resentment, inferiority, lies & ego.

The other is Good.

It is joy, peace, love, hope, humility, kindness, empathy, & truth."

The boy thought about it, and asked, "Grandfather, which wolf wins?"

The old man quietly replied, "*The one you feed.*"

These are not mystical forces outside us. They're tendencies within all of us. They shape how we speak, lead, decide, and respond. They shape the trajectory of our life, career, and relationships. Krishna's lens is diagnostic—a framework for transforming our habits of thought and action.

➤ *The battlefield isn't just around us—it's within us, moment by moment.*

In business, virtuous qualities like generosity, humility, self-discipline, inner calm, and non-violence are foundations of stable, conscious leadership. They create cultures that empower rather than intimidate. They inspire loyalty without demanding it.

➤ *Force may create compliance, but character builds trust.*

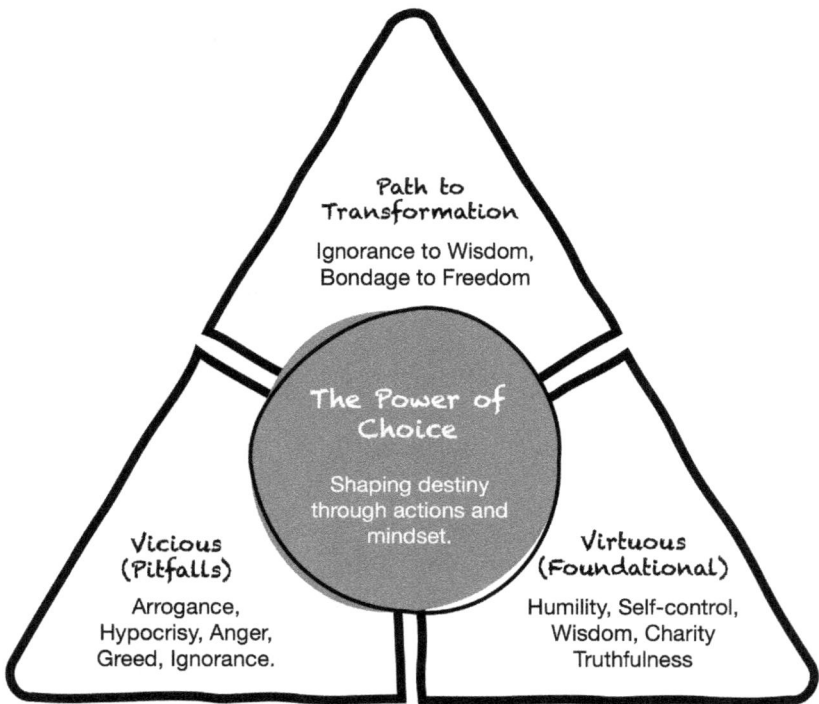

The vicious path, by contrast, manifests as manipulation, aggression, and impulsive gratification. It shows up as ego-driven leadership, short-term thinking, toxic culture, or ruthless decision-making. It may bring short-term results, but it destabilizes the system, harms others, and hollows out the self.

You are not to bury or suppress these vicious impulses but understand their roots—fear, insecurity, or unhealed scars—and transform them, redirect them. With reflection, anger becomes clarity, fear turns into courage, and restlessness becomes purposeful ambition.

➤ *The real transformation begins not by avoiding the negative but by consciously turning it into positive.*

By understanding the fork between virtuous and vicious paths, we gain the power to shape a character that frees us from distress and brings lasting peace. This is not an overnight fix but a steady refinement. One decision at a time, one response at a time, we grow into a better version of ourselves.

Playbook of Virtuous Qualities

Chapter 16, Verse 1: "Fearlessness, purity of heart, perseverance in yoga of knowledge, charity, sense restraint, sacrifice, study of scriptures, austerity, honesty..."

The virtuous qualities elevate character and expand impact. These are inner capacities: fearlessness, clarity, compassion, restraint, and humility. They are the foundation of real strength, shaping not just what we do (actions) but why we do it (motivations).

These qualities bring clarity amid chaos, integrity in uncertainty, and steadiness under pressure. While outer success often gets celebrated, it's these inner foundations that sustain impact and preserve balance.

They allow us to act without arrogance, succeed without exploitation, and grow without losing their ground.

➤ *Character isn't a strategy. It's your invisible edge.*

In leadership, they show up in how we handle conflict, power, deadlines, and people. They determine whether we *pull with purpose* or *push with fear*, whether we serve or control. When we pull with purpose without the desire to control, our teams feel safe, our choices feel aligned, and our growth feels earned.

Anchor Action in Wisdom with Discernment

Chapter 16, Verse 24: "Therefore, let the scriptures be your authority in assessing what should be done and what should not be done."

This is a reminder to act with discernment and inner clarity. The word "scripture" here symbolizes universal wisdom and timeless principles of truth, fairness, and integrity.

In personal life, ethics provide the foundation when circumstances demand action, but discernment helps us make grounded choices in real situations. The process is straightforward: (a) know your principles—the rules, written and unwritten, and (b) apply the layer of discernment to separate what's expedient from what's right. Then act with conviction.

➤ *Discernment doesn't slow you down—it keeps you from crashing.*

The business equivalent of "scriptural" guidance is ethical leadership, good governance, and adherence to enduring values.

They function as the moral compass to translate how decisions affect not just profits, but also people and the planet. Companies that prioritize fair labor, environmental stewardship, and honest dealings earn long-term trust. The pressure to bend rules can lead to moral compromises. Those who compromise these standards may see quick wins but eventually face reputational damage and erosion of stakeholder confidence.

➤ *When action is guided by principle, success becomes sustainable.*

The mantra is clear: Start from principles, not convenience—then let wisdom steer your choices. Principle sustains power. Clarity builds peace. Conscious action builds integrity. Doing the right thing, even when difficult, is not rigidity. It is wisdom in motion.

Entrepreneurial Framework 16:

The Character Compass: Business Integrity

Ethical entrepreneurs rise above destructive competition by prioritizing integrity, building trust, and creating value for all—while resisting greed and arrogance.

Theme: Playing the infinite game with integrity—grounded in principled clarity and the discernment to navigate right from wrong.

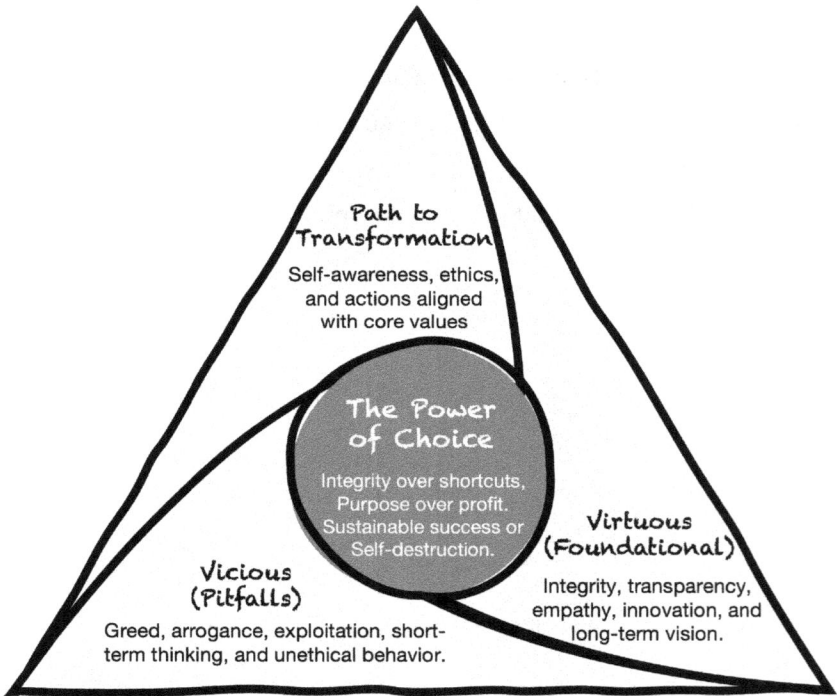

Path to Transformation
Self-awareness, ethics, and actions aligned with core values

The Power of Choice
Integrity over shortcuts, Purpose over profit. Sustainable success or Self-destruction.

Virtuous (Foundational)
Integrity, transparency, empathy, innovation, and long-term vision.

Vicious (Pitfalls)
Greed, arrogance, exploitation, short-term thinking, and unethical behavior.

Business Insight:

Business leadership is ultimately a test of character. Talent and strategy matter, but character is the invisible engine behind sustainable growth. The real differentiator over time is not charisma or genius but consistency, restraint, and trustworthiness.

144

▶ *In high-stakes environments, clarity of values outlasts clarity of vision.*

Many startups often race towards ambition and speed. But truly resilient ones are rooted in ethical clarity. Businesses thrive when they build trust on foundational virtues and pursue bold goals without compromising values. Leaders who rise above destructive competition by prioritizing integrity create organizations that grow sustainably and deliver value to all stakeholders.

▶ *Success is sustained by the strength of character behind the ambition.*

Companies that cut corners in pursuit of short-term profits often face backlash, regulatory scrutiny, and talent loss. Virtues don't weaken competitiveness—they sharpen it. Ethical guardrails don't restrict growth—they enable it.

The framework of virtuous and vicious qualities offers a powerful lens to evaluate leadership behavior as they shape what we build.

Warby Parker integrated a socially conscious mission with sustainable growth. Their *"Buy a Pair, Give a Pair"* program has provided millions of glasses to those in need—proving that ethics and ambition can scale together.

Action Step: When forks loom, turn within: "What holds our virtues?" "What might grind us down?" "What serves all?" Choose right, build trust, shape worth.

With **ethical leadership** in place, the next step is to **build trust and loyalty**, which is explored in the next chapter.

Chapter 17
Faith: The Driving Force Behind Our Actions

The seventeenth chapter of the *Gita*, opens with a powerful idea: faith shapes who we become. Our character, actions, and experiences are influenced by the nature of the faith we hold. Faith is not a spiritual or religious concept. Every person lives with a mind aligned to some form of faith. It is the result of influence absorbed from upbringing, culture, social interactions, or self-reflection. It shapes what we pursue, avoid, or tolerate.

▶ *Faith is not passive—it shapes our character in motion.*

There is a nuanced map between belief & behavior and intent & impact. Krishna classifies faith into three types based on the influence of the three primal energies. A leader who pursues growth with concern for people, ethics, and impact operates from *Sattvic* faith. One obsessed with chasing targets but blind to team health from burnout may be driven by *Rajasic* faith. A passive manager who clings to rituals or blame to let inefficiencies linger may reflect *Tamasic* faith.

Krishna makes another distinction—intent matters more in the expression of faith. Charity for applause, discipline to impress, or sacrifices from guilt are hollow performances when not backed by sincere intent. Impact comes from the intent, and when backed by conscious faith, it becomes transformative and changes the paradigm.

At work, when people follow rules, goals, or values mechanically without clarity of their intent, it creates disengagement. Leaders must pause and reflect—what is the *intent in the faith* behind their ambition, choices, or practices? A need to prove, a habit of performance, or a sense of service and purpose?

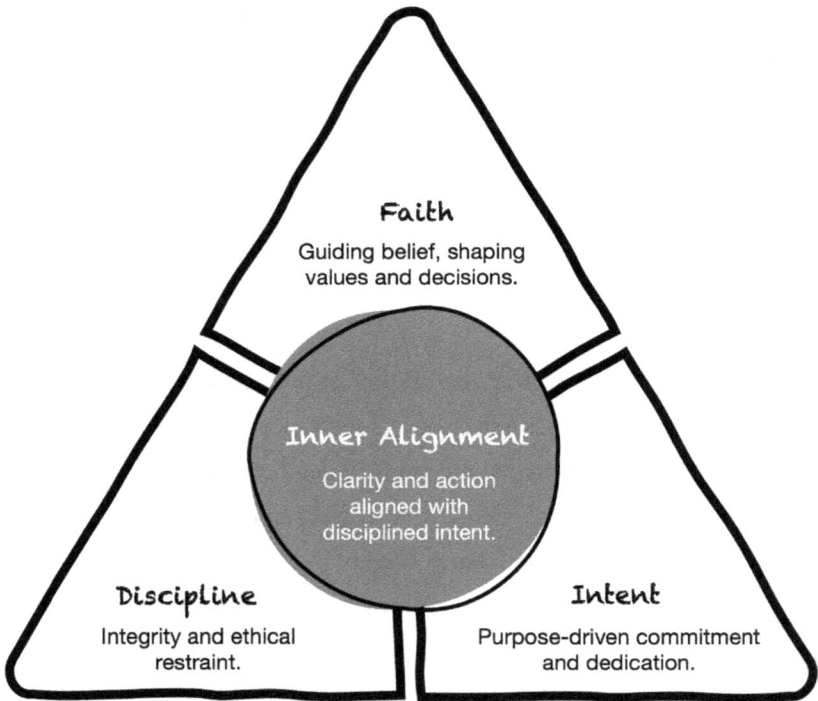

> ➤ *It's not just what you do. It's the intent you anchor it in that makes it real.*

This chapter is a call to refine the quality of faith that powers action. When we have faith with clarity, action becomes a means of growth, not exhaustion. Discipline, intent, and faith form the triangle of inner alignment; they become the foundation of conscious living and meaningful leadership.

True Austerity Must Be Selfless and Moderate

Chapter 17, Verse 5: "Those who practice severe austerities without following the prescription of the scriptures, motivated by hypocrisy and egotism, are impelled by their desire and attachment."

Austerity *(Tapa)* is conscious self-restraint for sharpening the mind, cultivating courage, deepening purpose, and nurturing inner strength. But when taken to extremes, fueled by pride, hypocrisy, or unnecessary hardship, it distorts rather than uplifts.

➤ *Austerity without discernment becomes self-inflicted punishment.*

In life, work, and business, austerity might show up as glorified overwork, rigid lifestyle routines, or performative sacrifices. Often leading to burnout, tunnel vision, and lost perspective. Leaders who enforce hardships and create pressure-cooker environments under the guise of mission create cultures of fear and resistance, stifling trust and innovation. Untethered from sincerity or purpose, it drains more than it delivers.

Balanced austerity is one that supports growth and ethical leadership without devolving into self-imposed hardship or glorifying hardship in pursuit of applause. Such a balance encourages learning, resilience, and sustainable success, guided by moderation and discernment.

➤ *Rigidity isn't strength—it's fragility in disguise.*

This is a call to reflect on and examine the intent behind our sacrifices. Do they expand our potential, or are they driven by the need to prove ourselves? Balanced austerity refines the self—it purifies and strengthens. It should elevate us, not exhaust us.

Faith Without Sincerity Is an Empty Ritual

Chapter 17, Verse 28: "Whatever is offered, given, practiced, or endured without faith is called 'false'—it holds no value in this life or the next."

This verse challenges the illusion of effort without devotion. Krishna's warning is unflinching: even the most lavish charity, sacrifice, or penance is an empty gesture if performed without faith. Actions devoid of genuine belief, no matter how grand or sacrificial, are ultimately unreal if the heart is hollow. Even austerity performed mechanically out of obligation bears no fruit, like seeds planted in barren soil.

► *Ritual without heart is noise—loud to the crowd, bankrupt before the Divine.*

In work, relationships, and life, we often mistake motion for meaning—burning ourselves out in rigid routines or clinging to tradition without questioning its relevance. Business leaders who demand blind compliance without inspiring shared purpose create cultures of disengagement. Organizations built on performance without purpose lose vitality.

Faith should be the lifeblood of action. Not blind belief, but sincerity that aligns our deeds with inner truth. It's the difference between a student memorizing answers vs. seeking understanding and a leader enforcing rules vs. modeling values.

150

➤ *Deeds done without faith leave no imprint—they pass but never transform.*

This verse is a mirror to our intentions: *Are we acting out of love or obligation? Offering to uplift or to impress?* True faith is demonstrated in the quiet integrity of why we do what we do. When action flows from that space, even the smallest deed becomes sacred.

Entrepreneurial Framework 17:

Faith, Trust & Loyalty in Business

A company's integrity is defined by the quality of its faith, which fuels the trust and loyalty of its customers, partners, employees, and even competitors.

Theme: Faith in long-term vision that builds trust and earns loyalty through transparency, fairness, and purpose.

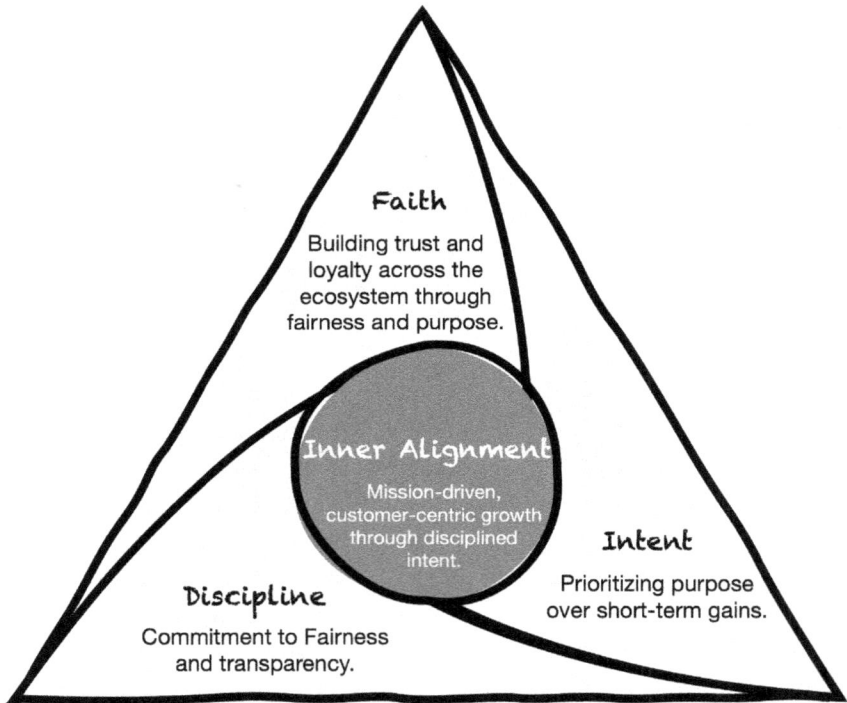

Faith
Building trust and loyalty across the ecosystem through fairness and purpose.

Inner Alignment
Mission-driven, customer-centric growth through disciplined intent.

Intent
Prioritizing purpose over short-term gains.

Discipline
Commitment to Fairness and transparency.

Business Insight:

At the heart of every enduring enterprise lies an unshakable foundation of *faith*—not merely as belief, but as active commitment to fairness and purpose. This principle radiates outward, building trust and loyalty across the entire business ecosystem: customers who become advocates, employees who grow into stewards, partners who transform into allies, and even competitors who respect the boundaries of principled competition.

Mission-driven organizations have a simple decision filter: *Does this honor our deeper purpose while serving stakeholder needs?* This is their compass, guiding them to build trust and loyalty. It comes through unwavering discipline in fairness and transparency—as non-negotiable practices, whether in pricing or policies. The crowning element is the intent that transforms routine operations into meaningful actions. *Are you selling products or solving problems? Managing employees or building teams? Trading with suppliers or building ecosystems?*

➤ *Faith isn't declared in vision statements—it's proven in how you act when no one's watching.*

In business, faith is about consistency. It is the invisible engine that powers trust, earns loyalty, and sustains reputation. A company's integrity is not declared in brand books—it's reflected in every decision, every delay, and every follow-through. The proof lives in companies that measure success not just by quarterly reports but by decades of earned trust and self-renewing loyalty.

When action flows from conscious intent, faith becomes visible, trust becomes inevitable, and loyalty becomes reciprocal.

Costco, for example, didn't earn employee and customer devotion through marketing or branding—but by consistently honoring fair pricing, shared value, and respect for workers. That's faith in action.

Action Step: When the calling is trust, ask yourself, "Does it serve our stakeholders?" "Is our process fair and transparent?" Strengthen conviction, act with integrity, and build lasting loyalty.

With **trust and loyalty** established, the final step is to **achieve liberated leadership**, which is explored in the next chapter.

Chapter 18
The Balance of Action and Ultimate Mastery

The eighteenth and culminating chapter of the *Gita*, Krishna weaves together themes of action, renunciation, detachment, purpose, and duty into a unified vision for ultimate clarity (*Moksha*), the inner liberation through renunciation. This is not a freedom from action but a freedom within it.

➤ *True freedom isn't withdrawal from the world—it's mastery within it.*

It is freedom from fear, ego, craving, and performance anxiety—this inner liberation enables clarity. Renunciation sets the stage with the surrender of inner compulsions. Not to walk away, but to walk free.

Renunciation is often misunderstood as different ways of *abandoning* action—whether through fear (*Tamasic*), frustration (*Rajasic*), or ethical ransom (*Sattvic*).

Krishna reframes renunciation not as escape but as evolution—the action continues, you remain engaged, but the ego's grip on the process dissolves. Here's what each type of renunciation means.

Tamasic is releasing the grip of delusion and inertia,
Rajasic is releasing the grip of attachment and impatience, and
Sattvic is releasing the rigidity of ethical analysis paralysis.

You <u>let go of what does not serve the purpose any longer</u>. Going from ego-driven action → ego-conscious action → ego-free action. At each stage, you're *more* engaged, not less. The action becomes purer, more spontaneous, more effective, as the ego steps back. It is the *freedom within action* rather than *freedom from action*.

➤ *True renunciation is refining action by releasing what doesn't serve.*

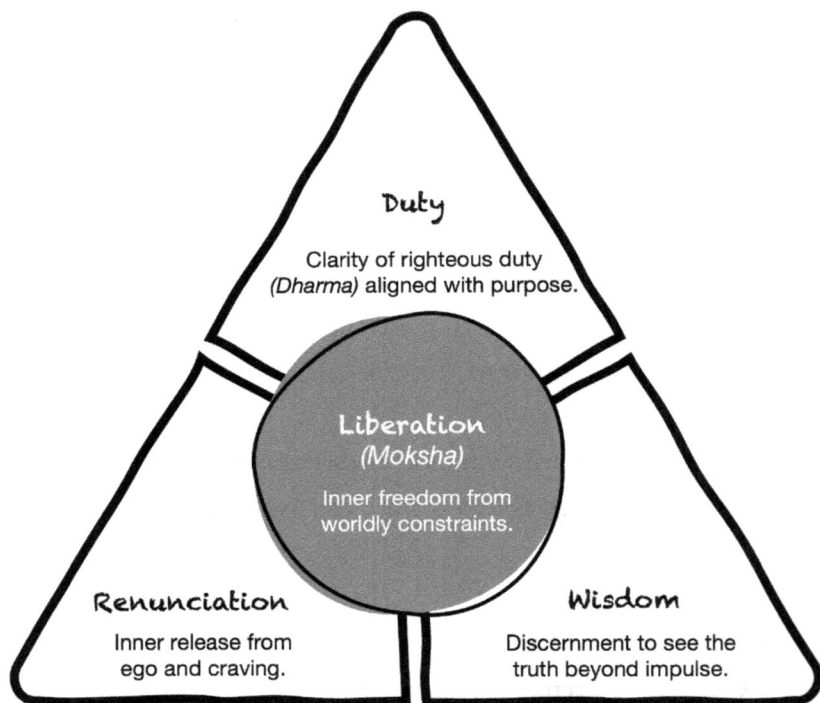

Duty

Clarity of righteous duty
(*Dharma*) aligned with purpose.

Liberation
(Moksha)

Inner freedom from
worldly constraints.

Renunciation

Inner release from
ego and craving.

Wisdom

Discernment to see the
truth beyond impulse.

With ego and craving released, and the lens of wisdom unobstructed, we gain the clarity to choose rightly—with the precision of surgical discernment. From that clarity comes the strength to recognize our purpose-driven duty *(Dharma)* and to pursue it with unshakable calm. When we act from *Duty*, anchored by *Wisdom* and *Renunciation*, we attain *Liberation*, the freedom within, and the clarity beyond (*Moksha*).

➤ *Inner freedom peaks when duty is clear, ego is released, and wisdom guides the way.*

This leads to a deeper idea: mastery lies in consistent, bold, and clear-sighted action, free from expectation. Whether leading a company or living a fulfilling life, impact is sustained when we fearlessly pursue excellence without being enslaved to results.

▶ *Mastery isn't leaving the battlefield—it's fighting without chains.*

This is where Mastery—what the Gita calls *Purusharth*—emerges: decisive, fearless, purpose-driven effort born from clarity and inner freedom. It's not frantic striving. It's calm intensity, rooted in inner steadiness and luminous with purpose. In business, it is the ability to make masterful moves to serve the mission, not to impress the markets. Vision with courage—action without emotional volatility.

▶ *Ambition without attachment. Action without anxiety. That's Purusharth.*

Here's how the *Gita's* great themes come together:

Action becomes purposeful when guided by **Duty**, stabilized by **Detachment**, cleared of ego by **Renunciation**, sparked by **Inner Freedom**, and turned into bold execution with **Mastery.**

Krishna also reminds us that *duty* must not be abandoned, even when difficult. A leader's responsibility isn't just performance—it's protecting purpose, people, and values, even under pressure. Leaders aligned with their deeper values become more than executives—they become stewards of trust, purpose, and service.

Character Matters More Than Birth

Chapter 18, Verse 42: "Peacefulness, self-control, austerity, purity, tolerance, honesty, transcendental knowledge, wisdom, and faith in the Supreme—these are natural duties of Brahmins, born of their inherent nature."

This verse is part of Krishna's discourse on social roles *(Varna)*, challenging the rigid notions of status and birth. He dismantles the idea that greatness is inherited. True glory comes not from lineage but from virtues: self-control, truth, inner balance, and knowledge.

It's a call for meritocracy. There is no entitlement, whether in business, work, or life. It translates into one clear message: *merit trumps privilege*. You don't need to be born into a business family to become an entrepreneur, nor do you need an Ivy League degree to rise as a CEO. What matters is who you choose to become—not where you started or where you came from.

➤ *Legacy isn't what you inherit. It's what you build.*

In a world wrestling with inequality and inherited advantage, cultures that prioritize competence and character over nepotism and hierarchies build innovation and trust—whether in companies or communities. Success is to be earned, not bestowed. It comes from continuous learning, grounded values, and authenticity. Krishna's verse celebrates this truth: <u>your character is your capital</u>.

➤ *Growth is not given—it's chosen. Every day.*

The message is clear: lasting success stems from your inner discipline, your courage to evolve, and your willingness to walk your path with purpose.

Wisdom in Action: The Path to Splendor and Morality

Chapter 18, Verse 78: "Wherever there is Krishna, the Lord of Yoga, wherever there is Arjun, the supreme archer, there will be splendor, victory, power, and morality."

This final verse is the Gita's mic drop. Victory belongs to those who unite *Krishna*—light of wisdom within—with *Arjun*—the arm of action. Strategy with execution. Vision with courage. Thoughtfulness with grit. This union of wisdom and action is **mastery**—the power to transform the battlefield of life into a ground for greatness.

▶ *It's not enough to know. It's not enough to do. The magic lies in doing with wisdom.*

In entrepreneurship, you may have the smartest idea in the world, but if you can't lead teams, make decisions, and execute under pressure, you'll fumble. Likewise, relentless hustle without clarity is wasted energy and burnout. So, *Strategy + Execution = Enduring Success.*

And yes, there's a moral dimension to it—victory means nothing if it's built on manipulation or compromise. Lasting power is that which uplifts—not just wins. So the *Gita's* formula is:
Strategy + Integrity + Execution = Enduring Success.

▶ *Victory without morality is empty. Power without purpose corrodes.*

This final verse isn't just closure. It's a call to live in alignment—to lead with clarity and act with courage. That's where splendor, victory, and enduring fulfillment arise.

Entrepreneurial Framework 18:

Liberated Leadership Mindset for Business Mastery

The pinnacle of entrepreneurial mastery is to lead with clarity and purpose, free from the anxieties of success or failure.

Theme: Mastery is the ability to lead with bold, decisive effort, fueled by inner freedom that comes from clarity.

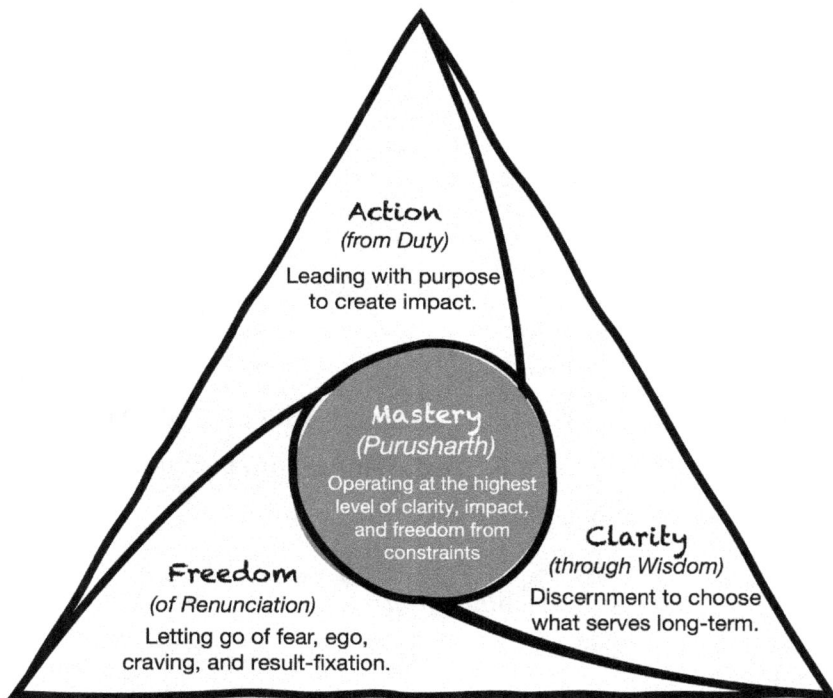

Action
(from Duty)
Leading with purpose to create impact.

Mastery
(Purusharth)
Operating at the highest level of clarity, impact, and freedom from constraints

Freedom
(of Renunciation)
Letting go of fear, ego, craving, and result-fixation.

Clarity
(through Wisdom)
Discernment to choose what serves long-term.

Business Insight:

At the apex of entrepreneurship, leaders don't scale faster—they scale deeper. This is the realm of **liberated leadership**, where the pursuit of *Mastery*—the bold and purposeful execution—is powered by the inner freedom that comes from *Clarity*.

➤ *Clarity purifies the intent. Mastery manifests the impact.*

Clarity frees you from the tyranny of fear, applause, and ego that clears the fog. It asks, "What really matters?" *Mastery* is precision in motion. It says, "Now act like it matters." It transforms clarity into courageous execution—the state from which exceptional entrepreneurs operate. You pivot without panic. You build with presence, not pressure. This is where mastery lives—not in scaling noise, but in deepening signal.

➤ *Clarity, not control. Detachment, not disengagement. Intent, not applause. This leads to Mastery.*

How they work in tandem:
- *Clarity* whispers, "You are not your outcomes."
- *Mastery* commands, "Then let's make them matter."

This isn't a balance. It's alchemy. Clarity provides the *why*. Mastery delivers the *how*. Together, they turn startups into institutions and founders into stewards of meaning.

Without *Clarity, Mastery* becomes <u>*motion without meaning*</u>.
Without *Mastery, Clarity* becomes <u>*contemplation without consequence*</u>.

Only their fusion creates companies that endure economically, culturally and ethically.

• **Satya Nadella** at Microsoft: He didn't just steer a pivot from a product-centric company to a cloud and AI-driven future—he liberated the culture, the business model, and the company's future. A case study in liberated leadership.

162

• **Howard Schultz** at Starbucks: When he returned in 2008, he didn't just fix operations—he reignited the company's soul with *Clarity*, which then fueled global expansion with *Mastery*.

Mastery in business is the ability to lead with freedom, make bold decisions, and drive meaningful impact while navigating the complex maze of external forces without being controlled by them. This is the state where clarity, detachment, and purpose-driven leadership come together to build businesses that endure beyond the individual and drive meaningful transformation.

This is where the *Gita's* quiet revolution of Purposeful Mastery becomes a business playbook for generations. Where the *inner transformation of clarity* meets *outer contribution of mastery* to build lives and businesses that are truly significant.

Action Step: "When clarity reigns, stand tall: "What hones our vision?" "What fuels our reach?" "What marks our rise?" You lead free, cut sharp, build bold.

The Synergy of Clarity and Mastery for Purposeful Success

Clarity is inner (personal) liberation—it is the mastery of self *(Moksha)*, while *Mastery* drives the outer impact, the legacy of purposeful effort in the world *(Purusharth)*.

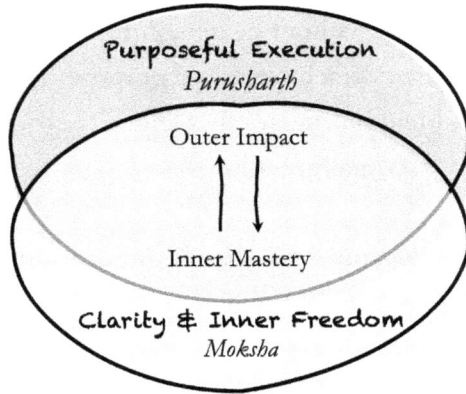

➤ *Inner mastery sustains outer legacy. The Gita's wisdom shows us how to build both.*

This is where the *Gita's* quiet revolution of Purposeful Mastery becomes a life and business playbook for generations. When inner transformation meets outer contribution, we build lives and businesses that are not only successful but significant. This synergy of *Clarity* and *Mastery* is a virtuous cycle, where inner fulfillment fuels outward impact, and outward impact reinforces inner growth. This is the essence of living the *Gita's* wisdom.

➤ *Clarity cuts through noise. Mastery cuts through resistance.*

Closing Reflections
The Entrepreneur's Lamp

As you embark on your path of mastery, remember that it requires rhythm. And rhythm comes from regular practice, and it requires energy that is directed, sustained, and aligned.

Ideas without action don't lift off. Drive without alignment leads to drift. Structure without motion leads to decay. What's needed is balance.

The sweet spot? The right mix of vision, energy, and containment:
Vision and values to know what matters
Focused execution to drive what's next
Stillness and structure to hold it all together

Awareness is the first step. Practice is next.

To help you with that, here's your daily practice of mastery—The Entrepreneur's Lamp.

The Entrepreneur's Lamp is a metaphor and a daily reflection practice to help you balance the three primal energies or forces that shape your presence and performance—your vision, your drive, and your capacity to recover. Each plays a role. When these align, you build with intention. When they don't, you burn out, stall, or chase shadows.

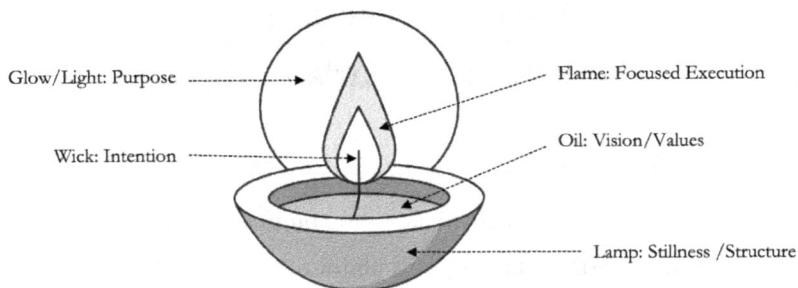

Glow/Light: Purpose — Flame: Focused Execution — Wick: Intention — Oil: Vision/Values — Lamp: Stillness /Structure

The Entrepreneur's Lamp is a practice to tune your internal state before you engage with the external world. It is built of four elements. Together, they sustain your light:

1. **Oil** (Vision and Values): *I am the truth in the golden glow.*

The oil fuels the flame. It is your purpose and your principles. *The Oil draws from the Path of Knowledge and the Path of Devotion. Ethics with purpose. Commitment without attachment.*

Ask yourself: *What pain or friction does my work reduce? What purpose does it serve?* Write it in one sentence. Then define your three non-negotiable ethical boundaries. They contain your fuel—keep it clean.

Example: *My work reduces hiring chaos for fast-growing startups.* Boundaries: *No misleading metrics. No copy-paste culture. No talent shortcuts.*

2. **Wick** (Intention): *I am the will that turns oil into light.*

Intention bridges purpose and action. *The Wick anchors attention to what matters today.*

Each morning, visualize the wick carrying the oil to turn it into a glow. Speak your intention aloud: *Today, I fuel [goal] with [action].*

Example: *Today, I fuel the <u>building of the sales pipeline</u> with <u>3 outreach calls</u>.*

3. **Flame** (Focused Execution): *I burn bright but never to ashes.*

This is your execution energy. Burn focused, not frantic.
The Flame draws strength from the Path of Focus and the Path of Action, powered by Devotion. It channels will into movement without burnout.

Structure your day in 90-minute bursts of high-intensity work. Then pause for 10 minutes. *Breathe. Reflect. Reset.*

Mantra: *I am the flame, not the ash.*

4. **Lamp** (Stillness and Structure): *I am the vessel for light to dance eternal.*

Stillness is not laziness. It's containment, holding everything in balance. A lamp without form spills.
The Lamp draws on the Path of Intellect and the Path of Focus. It brings discipline to your reflection and holds your energy steady.

Make space for grounding. A walk, a journal, a deliberate stop. Daily reset: 1 hour outdoors. No agenda. Just space to hold the fire.

When the Lamp Flickers: Troubleshooting

Oil too thick: You are overidealizing. **Apply the 1% Experiment.** What's one small thing you can test, even if it challenges your beliefs or feels uncomfortable?

Wick too weak: You are doubting or dragging. **Express your fears.** When spoken aloud, fear loses power. Speak to a mentor, a journal, or yourself.

Erratic flame: You are burning out. **Bring back rhythm.** Cadence protects intensity. Include moments of calm, reflection, and conviction.

The Lamp's True Purpose

A lamp doesn't cook. It shouldn't scorch or burn. Your lamp converts oil into radiance to turn darkness into light. Its purpose is simply to illuminate.

To use this flame for aggression (burning competitors) or greed (overheating growth) is to mistake a lamp for a weapon. Your purpose is to shine consistently, not to out-burn others.

This practice is your reminder:
- Build from purpose.
- Act with intention.
- Burn with rhythm.
- Protect your vessel.

Let the lamp stay lit.

Living the Gita: From Insight to Impact

As we conclude this journey from mediocrity to mastery, remember this book is a distilled guide to the *Gita's* most vital teachings, offered as a practical companion to navigating modern life and leadership. The *Gita's* 700 verses contain an ocean of timeless wisdom, and what you've explored here is an invitation to its depths.

The intent was never to dissect every philosophical nuance. Instead, it was to extract and apply practical wisdom—insights that can be lived, built upon, and turned into meaningful action. If it has sparked a fresh lens on how you work, lead, grow, or serve, then this journey has met its purpose.

The *Gita* is not a book to be read once and set aside. It offers us a framework to navigate life's complexities by understanding the interplay of forces that shape our decisions and emotions. The triangular representations introduced throughout this book are not just visual aids—they are mental models. They help translate the *Gita's* teachings into practical tools for daily decision-making and conscious living.

▶ *Success fades. Significance endures.*

Begin Your Journey of Transformation

The *Gita* is ultimately about mastery over oneself, over desires, and over the chaos of the mind. It doesn't ask us to abandon ambition but to elevate it with purpose. It doesn't demand withdrawal, but wiser engagement. Its real promise? To act with power and peace, without attachment or fear.

This journey is your starting point, not your conclusion. The insights here are tools to guide your own inquiry, your own evolution. The *Gita's* wisdom is timeless, and its true power lies not just in contemplation but in application. So, embark on the path of transformation. Reflect on the frameworks. Apply the teachings to your decisions.

➤ *Contemplation reveals the path. Application transforms the journey.*

Now it is your turn to embody these teachings to lead a life of fulfillment, impact, and enduring success.

Your Gita begins here.

Your journey Beyond Mediocrity.

Every decision is your next verse.

Every action is your sacred practice.

Walk with clarity. Build with courage.

The world awaits your Dharma in motion.

www.ingramcontent.com/pod-product-compliance
Lightning Source LLC
Chambersburg PA
CBHW071642210326
41597CB00017B/2080